The New
SuperLeadership

Other Books by Charles C. Manz and Henry P. Sims, Jr.

The Wisdom of Solomon at Work:
Ancient Virtues for Living and Leading Today
Charles C. Manz, Karen P. Manz, Robert D. Marx, and Christopher P. Neck
Berrett-Koehler, 2001

Team Work and Group Dynamics
Gregory Stewart, Charles C. Manz, and Henry P. Sims, Jr.
Wiley, 1999

Mastering Self-Leadership
Charles C. Manz and Christopher Neck
Prentice-Hall, 1992; 2nd ed., 1999

The Leadership Wisdom of Jesus
Charles C. Manz
Berrett-Koehler, 1998; paperback 1999

For Team Members Only
Charles C. Manz, Christopher Neck, James Mancuso, and Karen P. Manz
AMACOM, 1997

Company of Heroes:
Unleashing the Power of Self-Leadership
Henry P. Sims, Jr., and Charles C. Manz
Wiley, 1996

Business Without Bosses: How Self-Managing Teams
Are Building High Performing Companies
Charles C. Manz and Henry P. Sims, Jr.
Wiley, 1993; paperback 1995

The New Leadership Paradigm
Henry P. Sims, Jr., and Peter Lorenzi
Sage, 1992

SuperLeadership: Leading Others to Lead Themselves
Charles C. Manz and Henry P. Sims, Jr.
Prentice-Hall, 1989; Berkley Books, 1990 (paperback)

The Thinking Organization
Henry P. Sims, Jr., and Dennis Gioia
Jossey Bass, 1986

The Art of Self-Leadership
Charles C. Manz
Prentice-Hall, 1983

The New SuperLeadership

LEADING OTHERS TO LEAD THEMSELVES

Charles C. Manz
and Henry P. Sims, Jr.

BERRETT-K

Berrett-Koehler Publishers, Inc.
450 Sansome Street, Suite 1200
San Francisco, CA 94111-3320
Tel: (415) 288-0260 Fax: (415) 362-2512 www.bkconnection.com

Ordering Information
Quantity sales. Special discounts are available on quantity purchases by corporations, associations, and others. For details, contact the "Special Sales Department" at the Berrett-Koehler address above.
Individual sales. Berrett-Koehler publications are available through most bookstores. They can also be ordered direct from Berrett-Koehler: Tel: (800) 929-2929; Fax: (802) 864-7626; www.bkconnection.com
Orders for college textbook/course adoption use. Please contact Berrett-Koehler: Tel: (800) 929-2929; Fax: (802) 864-7626.
Orders by U.S. trade bookstores and wholesalers. Please contact Publishers Group West, 1700 Fourth Street, Berkeley, CA 94710. Tel: (510) 528-1444; Fax: (510) 528-3444.

Printed in the United States of America
Printed on acid-free and recycled paper that is composed of 50% recovered fiber, including 10% post consumer waste.

Library of Congress Cataloging-in-Publication Data
Manz, Charles C.
        The new superleadership leading others to lead themselves / Charles C.
Manz and Henry P. Sims.
            p. cm.
        ISBN 1-57675-105-8
        1. Leadership. I. Sims, Henry P., 1939– II. Title.
        HD57.7 .M388 2000
        658.4'092—dc21
                                                                        00-012726

First Edition
06 05 04 03 02 01 00   10 9 8 7 6 5 4 3 2 1

Interior Design & Illustration: Gopa Design & Illustration
Copy Editor: Sandra Beris
Indexer: Paula C. Durbin-Westby
Proofreader: Henrietta Bensussen
Production: Linda Jupiter, Jupiter Productions

Dedicated to our daughters and sons

Katy and Chris
and
Amy, Andrew, and Jonathan

*The persons who have contributed most to our practical
understanding of the challenges of leading others
to lead themselves*

Table of Contents

PART III
SuperLeadership—It's In the Details

PART IV
SuperLeadership in the 21st Century

Acknowledgments

IN PREPARING THIS BOOK we have been fortunate to have had many sources of inspiration and support. We recognize the continuing inspiration of many individuals that have over the years contributed to our thinking about empowering leadership that brings out the self-leadership in others, including Harold Angle, Chris Argyris, Barry Bateman, Michael Beyerlein, Alan Cheney, Richard Cherry, Tom Cummings, Samer Faraj, Dennis Gioia, Richard Hackman, Peter Hom, Robert House, Ed Lawler, Ted Levitt, Ed Locke, Peter Lorenzi, Kathi Lovelace, Fred Luthans, Bary Macy, Mike Mahoney, Jim Mancuso, Karen Manz, Bob Marx, Chris Neck, John Newstrom, Craig Pearce, Tom Peters, Phil Podsakoff, Frank Shipper, Laurie Sims, Greg Stewart, Skip Szalagyi, Linda Trevino, and Seokhwa Yun. All of these people have significantly affected our thinking and writing over the years. We appreciate Richard Cherry's mentorship and help during the early stages of our research about teams. We continue to appreciate Tom Peters' contribution of a foreword for our original SuperLeadership book. We especially express our appreciation to our colleagues that helped us with the preparation of the various leadership profiles throughout the book, including Vikas Anand, Elliott Carlisle, Don Harrison, Narda Quigley, Ken A. Smith, Abhishek Srivastava, and Seokhwa Yun. Indeed, without their efforts much of this book would not exist. Many of these co-authors were the "experts" and/or key links that were critical to the process of developing the inside information for each of the stories.

We are also very grateful to the many others that helped make the writing and printing of this book a reality. We thank all the helpful people at Berrett-Koehler Publishers. We especially thank Steven Piersanti, our editor, who effectively challenged us to make this a better book.

In addition we thank our respective universities, the University of Massachusetts-Amherst (especially the Isenberg School of Management) and The University of Maryland-College Park (especially the Robert. H. Smith College of Business), for their support of our research and writing over the years. Our thanks extend to our deans and chairs: Tom O'Brien, Linda Smircich, Rudy Lamone, Bert Leete, Howard Frank, Ed Locke, Susan Taylor, and Ken G. Smith. We especially appreciate the support for manuscript preparation provided by the Administrative Support Center at the Isenberg School of Management at the University of Massachusetts. Ms. Becky Jerome provided superb support in preparing the manuscript.

Charles Manz would like to offer a special thanks to Charles and Janet Nirenberg whose generous gift made his current position as the Nirenberg professor of Business Leadership possible. He would also like to acknowledge the support of the Harvard Business School, which awarded him a Marvin Bower Fellowship for 1988–1989, the time period in which the final touches were completed for the original *SuperLeadership* volume.

We also owe a special thanks to the companies and managers and employees whose inspiration our many examples and profiles draw upon in order to paint vivid realistic pictures of SuperLeadership in action.

Finally, we thank our families and especially our wives, Karen and Laurie. The energy we have been able to spend writing this and our other books and articles has been greatly facilitated by their support and understanding. Hank Sims thanks his father, the original and real Henry P. Sims, for his lifelong inspiration to his loving family.

Introduction:
A Call for SuperLeadership

"Give a man a fish, and he will be fed for a day;

teach a man to fish, and he will be fed for a lifetime."

EVERYONE HAS HEARD THIS EXPRESSION, and the logic underlying this book is similar. We might paraphrase: "Be a strong, even a charismatic leader and followers will know where to go as long as you light their way. Teach them to lead themselves, and their path will be lighted always." And we would add, "In return, they will illuminate new paths of opportunity that you might have never seen."

A number of years ago we coined the term "SuperLeadership" to describe leadership that helps others to lead themselves. Given the wave of demand for individual empowerment that was beginning to sweep the country at that time, this concept struck a strong chord with the public, especially with business executives. We believed strongly that SuperLeadership filled a critical void in understanding how leadership could help meet the challenge of successfully putting empowerment into practice in organizations.

As we move onward into the 21st century we believe that Super-Leadership is needed even more today than it was then. For most organizations, empowerment is no longer a new management fad but a requirement for survival. And as more and more people work remotely and independently with the aid of advanced information technology, and as the world continues to become increasingly complex, changing, and globally integrated, the call for a new kind of leadership is echoing through the virtual halls of the new knowledge-based corporations. We believe this call again beckons Super-Leadership to move to center stage.

A Brief History of SuperLeadership

SuperLeadership: Leading Others to Lead Themselves was originally published in 1989, was well received, and went on to become a bestseller. We were pleased that management guru Tom Peters contributed a foreword. (See excerpts in the following box.) The book was awarded the Stybel-Peabody literary prize and was chosen to be a feature selection in the Executive Book Club. An audiotape version was published by the widely distributed Fast Track series. A year later, a paperback version was published and became a bestseller. *SuperLeadership* also received significant media attention, being featured on television and radio as well as in many magazines and newspapers across the country. The book was also published in several foreign language editions.

Most of all, we found the acceptance by the managerial and executive community to be dramatically positive and exceptionally gratifying. *SuperLeadership* has significantly impacted practice and training in organizations of all sizes. Many of these have been *Fortune* 500 companies, some of which distributed material from the book, or the book itself, on a widespread basis to employees throughout their organizations. Others used the SuperLeadership and self-leadership concepts and strategies as a key component of their leadership and empowerment efforts and training programs.

SuperLeadership challenges our fundamental assumptions about leadership and offers a powerful alternative for unleashing the vast capabilities of others.

In the past ten years we have personally delivered hundreds of speeches and executive development modules on the topic of Super-Leadership. The single overwhelming response from managers and executives has been a simultaneous fascination with how Super-Leadership challenges the fundamental assumptions that they have learned about leadership, and yet offers a powerful alternative for

> In SuperLeadership, Charles Manz and Hank Sims . . . focus on leaders who lead, not for their own edification and glory, not through command and authority, but through a subtle and ill-understood process that leads others to *lead themselves* to excellence. Indeed, in reading *SuperLeadership*, I recognized many of the characteristics that they articulate in the numerous executives I had encountered in researching my books.
>
> Manz's and Sims's book has a further strength. The authors do a superb job of articulating specific behaviors and strategies that leaders can use to bring out excellence in others. While philosophy and abstract vision are important executive strengths, the actions that executives take to realize these visions are critical. *SuperLeadership* is action-oriented—it proposes specific strategies for leading others to lead themselves.
>
> I remain convinced that executive leadership will continue to be the critical ingredient in the success or failure of American business and industry. Certainly, the corporate environment is becoming more complex and transitory, so the more we can understand about leadership, the more effective our business organizations can be. Understanding *SuperLeadership* moves us closer to this elusive goal.
>
> —Tom Peters, from the Foreword to *SuperLeadership*, 1989

unleashing the vast capabilities of their followers. The concept appears to move them to take a penetrating look in the mirror, which helps free them to empower others while moving themselves toward becoming highly effective leaders—SuperLeaders. Many seem to realize for the first time that the best measure of their own leadership effectiveness is not how much they personally excel and receive acclaim. Instead, the effectiveness of leadership can be measured by the success of others.

SUPERLEADERSHIP: EVEN MORE IMPORTANT FOR THE 21ST CENTURY

When most people think of leadership, they think of one person doing something to another person. We call this "influence" and we think of a leader as one who has the ability to influence another. A classic leader—one whom everyone recognizes *is* a leader—is sometimes described as "charismatic" or "heroic." A popular concept is the idea of a "transformational" leader, one who has the vision and dynamic personal attraction to generate total organizational change. The word *leader* itself conjures up visions of a striking figure on a rearing white horse, crying "follow me!" The leader is the one who has power, authority, or charisma enough to command others.

We think of the historical figures who fit this mold: Alexander the Great, Caesar, Napoleon, George Washington, Churchill, Patton. Even Lee Iacocca's turnaround of Chrysler Corporation might be thought of as a notable example of 20th century heroic leadership in a manufacturing organization. More recently, Steven Jobs accomplished a similar feat in a high-tech environment after returning as CEO of the then financially troubled Apple Computer. It's not difficult to imagine Iacocca or Jobs astride a white horse, riding out in front of the troops at Chrysler or Apple.

But is this heroic leadership figure the most appropriate role model for the organizational leader of the 21st century? What kind of leader is needed for an information-based organization that operates in a rapidly changing world? How can highly independent and physically dispersed telecommuters be effectively led? What kind of leadership is appropriate for leading empowered team members who are supposed to be leading themselves? Is there another model? We believe there is.

We begin with the idea that true leadership comes mainly from within a person, not from outside. At its best, external leadership can provide a spark and support the flame of the powerful self-leadership that dwells within each person. At its worst, it disrupts this internal process, damaging the person and creating conflicts between inner and external influences.

This perspective demands that we come up with a new measure of leadership strength—the ability to maximize the contributions of others by helping them to effectively guide their own destinies, rather than the ability to bend the will of others. We refer to this subtle yet tremendously powerful approach to leadership as *Super-Leadership—leading others to lead themselves*.

SuperLeaders marshal the strength of many, for their strength does not lie solely in their own abilities but in the vast, multiple talents of those who surround them. In this sense, the word super has a different connotation than it does in comic books, or in terms like superman or supermom. It does concern bringing out the best—but mainly in others, not just the leader. The SuperLeader does not try to carry the weight of a hyperchanging high-tech world alone, but shares this burden with others. And those others become stronger and stronger through their initiative, creativity, and real contributions. As others become stronger, the leader gains the strength of the unleashed potential of many, and consequently can become a SuperLeader.

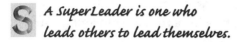

A SuperLeader is one who leads others to lead themselves.

Our underlying philosophy is optimistic. We believe in the vast, often hidden capability within leaders and their followers. Super-Leadership taps the potential of each person to make the world a better place, if given a chance. This is crucial in a world of accelerating change, where knowledge workers need to contribute their fuller potential, where no one person can know it all and make all the decisions competently on their own. We believe that Super-Leadership confronts the demands of the 21st century head on. It provides a road map for meeting vast challenges and opportunities in a way in which everyone can be involved and, in a very real sense, everyone can be a leader.

So What's New this Time?
Leadership in the Age of Information

First, let's make it clear, this book is deeply rooted in the original version, *SuperLeadership*, published in 1989 and 1990. We are faithful to our own original ideas and rhetoric. But indeed, there are many changes to this new book for the 21st century.

Over the years we have developed an enriched model of how SuperLeadership can actually be implemented. In many ways the actual practice of leadership by real executives in real organizations has changed dramatically over the last decade, mainly toward the ideas represented by *SuperLeadership*. It's becoming easier to find real life SuperLeaders such as Dennis Bakke of AES (see later profile). We have observed and recorded this change, and much of it is reflected in our new writing.

Our views of self-leadership have been enriched and expanded, and this is also reflected in this new book. We have given special emphasis to the ideas of expressing self-leadership through seeking out the natural rewards in work, and by influencing one's own patterns of thinking. Our current thinking and writing reflects a holistic, integrative perspective that recognizes the interrelated role of behavior, thought, and emotion for effectively leading ourselves. Self-leadership is truly the heart of SuperLeadership and receives a great deal of attention in this book.

Practical self-leadership consists of both action- and mind-focused strategies designed to enhance personal achievement and effectiveness. We especially draw upon the thinking that Charles Manz brought forth in his recent book with Christopher Neck, *Mastering Self-Leadership* (2nd edition).

S *SELF-LEADERSHIP—a philosophy and a systematic set of actions and mental strategies for leading ourselves to higher performance and effectiveness.*

Many of the changes in the book are focused on the examples, cases, and profiles that we use. We have many new examples and profiles that reflect more contemporary leadership, especially in high-tech and knowledge-based environments.

Perhaps the most prominent change is the way we have incorporated the realities of the information age into this new version. In the first and last chapters especially, we have articulated the dramatic, cutting-edge changes in communication and information processing and what these changes mean for leadership in the 21st century. We believe that the age of information will require more and more investment in human capital, and that SuperLeadership is the way to bring out the best in the people who inhabit our organizations of the 21st century.

The most important change is the emphasis on how the age of information has changed leadership and made self-leadership an essential skill for everyone.

SOME SUPERLEADERSHIP THEMES

Here are some primary themes that capture the spirit of the book:

- Given the rapid change, complexity, and new high-tech autonomous work roles of the information age, SuperLeadership is needed even more now than it was in the past.

- SuperLeaders lead others to lead themselves.

- The first critical step of SuperLeadership is to master self-leadership.

- Superleaders establish values, model, encourage, reward, and in many other ways foster self-leadership in individuals, teams, and wider organizational cultures.

Some expressions that illustrate the above themes include:

- An important measure of a leader's own success is the success of others.

- "[This transition to SuperLeadership] is even more difficult for me than other people . . . I started to realize that I better let some other people do some things and I better start looking at the big picture a little more."—Joseph Vincent Paterno

- The strength of a leader is measured by the ability to facilitate the self-leadership of others—not the ability to bend the will of others to the leaders.

- If leaders want to lead somebody, they must first lead themselves.

▶ The best of all leaders is the one who helps people so that eventually they don't need him or her.

The stories, examples, and cases used throughout this book are designed to provide practical insight on how SuperLeadership can be used successfully by leaders. But the most important point is to understand the underlying philosophy—that is, as a leader you *can* act to enhance and unleash the self-leadership of others. In the process, you will become a SuperLeader!

Part I

The Ghosts of Leadership:
Past, Present, and Future

Leadership in the 21st Century

A leader is best

When people barely know he exists,

Not so good when people obey and acclaim him,

Worse when they despise him.

But of a good leader, who talks little,

When his work is done, his aim fulfilled,

They will say:

We did it ourselves.

—Lao Tzu

OW DOES THIS PERSPECTIVE FIT with your own ideas about leadership? Do you feel comfortable with the idea that a leader should not be obeyed or acclaimed, and in fact should barely be recognized? When you are called upon to lead do you prefer to take charge or to help others find their own way? These timeless words of Lao Tzu were written well over 2,000 years ago, yet they send an important message worth considering as we enter a new age. The recent end of the millennium seems particularly symbolic. We are living on the cusp of one of those rare technological turning points in history. Over the past two decades the information revolution emphasized computers and software. But this was only prologue to the main event—the Internet. Mankind is becoming truly "connected" and life will never be the same.

Of course, this revolution in information has substantial ramifications for our social systems. As one example, the way many of us go about our daily work has changed radically because of one communication capability: e-mail. Our patterns of daily work are just very different than they were ten years ago. And it will change further—e-mail is going wireless. The initial technology is already here; by 2010 most of us will have the capability to be connected wherever we are, wherever we go, whenever we want.

But this is a book about leadership—how one person influences others. How will the technological revolution change the nature of leadership? We believe the effect will be extensive and profound. We are in the midst of a vastly changing social fabric where technology is transforming business, family structures, schools, governments, and even religious institutions. Indeed, all of us face a very challenging arena for exercising leadership in the 21st century.

 As only one example, how does one person lead another when that person is located at a remote place?

In this book, we propose a different form of leadership, one that emphasizes the empowerment of others. We call this form of leadership *SuperLeadership*—that is, leading others to lead themselves.

The industrial age with its hierarchical command-and-control form of organizing is past. The information revolution is causing the deconstruction of organizations. That is, hierarchy is no longer needed to filter and facilitate the movement of information required for task integration. Instead, agents of the organization can now communicate directly and with greater speed, flexibility, and effectiveness.

The key to organizational success . . . will be to have the right person solving the most important business problems, no matter where they are located in the company hierarchically, organizationally, or geographically.

—James Citrina and Thomas Neff[1]

Of course, this requires that people possess the skills and knowledge to conduct their information-rich transactions in a speedy manner. The true assets of organizations will no longer be bricks and mortar, but the knowledge invested in their human capital.

And how do we lead these knowledge workers? We believe first that the ultimate control comes from within—that the essence of leadership in today's information age is to develop the capacity of people to lead themselves. The real challenge is to maximize the potential of human capital by unleashing this inner self-leadership. The most effective leader of the 21st century will be a SuperLeader, one who leads others to lead themselves in the information age.

As a quick preview, consider the following sample of distinctive strategies of a SuperLeader that will be presented throughout this book:

- Listen more and talk less.

- Ask more questions and give fewer answers.

- Foster learning from mistakes, not fear of consequences.

- Encourage problem solving by others rather than solving problems for others.

- Share information rather than hoard it.

- Encourage creativity, not conformity.

- Encourage teamwork and collaboration, not destructive competition.

- Foster independence and interdependence, not dependence.

- Develop committed self-leaders, not compliant followers.

- Lead others to lead themselves, not to be under the control of others.

▶ Establish organizational structures that support self-leadership, such as self-managing teams, virtual teams, distance working.

▶ Establish information systems through the Intranet and Internet that will support self-leadership.

▶ Establish a holistic self-leading culture throughout the organization.

THE TECHNOLOGICAL REVOLUTION

Think about the typical organizational employee of the 21st century. More specifically, Consider the situation of Alica, a 30-year-old consultant who is indeed "connected."

Alica has a desktop at home and also works with a 2.5 lb. lightweight laptop with a full size keyboard and screen, although she finds herself using the voice recognition routine more than the keyboard.

But the real jewel in her array of devices is her communication platform—an all-in-one lightweight device about the size of today's palm computers, but one that has 100 times the computing power of today's Pentium III desktop. This device is a computer, PDA, cell phone, and even has a mini-videoconferencing capacity.

The device is made by Nokia and is an advanced version of the so-called "3G" family of all-purpose communication devices, sometimes known as the Universal Mobile Telephone System, or UMTS. Voice conversation is just one of its many capabilities. Of course, the Nokia has Internet capabilities, voice recognition, and also wireless synchronization with Alica's desktop and laptop computers. The screen is a color display that provides entry to her personal calendar, news, Internet, Intranet, address book, personal files, etc. She uses a small wireless "ear bud" to receive transmissions, but so far she has refused to have the "implant" behind her ear that would make reception and transmission instantaneous.

At home and in the office she is connected by broadband, a communication protocol that seems like instantaneous transfer to her. She is easily able to transfer information from one device to any other.

As a consultant, Alica is mainly engaged in "information work" and some would call her a "knowledge worker." (Michael Dertouzos defines information work as "the transformation of information by human brains or computer programs."[2] In 1997, Dertouzos estimated that 50 to 60 percent of an industrialized country's GNP consists of information work. Clearly, this will continue to increase significantly.)

Alica has one place that she prefers to do "alone" type work. This place is her home, and this is where she still uses some old-fashioned books and paper materials. But most of her personal reference data is stored on her personal file system and is accessible wherever she is. And of course she has the powerful research tool represented by her company's Intranet and the larger, more public Internet.

Alica does not have a real office outside her home. Since she is a consultant, her office typically is a transitory place located at her client's venue, a broadband-wired hotel room or a "drop in" office. She is a walking, talking, data-receiving-and-sending communication entity.

Alica is a member of several teams or task forces, although she seldom meets with a team as a whole. On a day-to-day basis they typically communicate through their various systems. But most of her teams try to meet on occasion to do some personal bonding.

Despite all this technical augmentation, she values face-to-face opportunities and worries about becoming captured and consumed by the technology. She is concerned about privacy because she knows that with her communication platform, her actual physical location is available to others. Most of all she wants a high degree of control and discretion about where, when, and how she goes about doing her job. She wants to come and go when and where she desires, and uses the communication technology to help her do this. She also has a keen sense of dressing the way she wants versus knowing when and where to "wear the costume."

She frequently asks "why" and expects an answer. She wants to be evaluated and rewarded on the basis of end results rather than how she got there. She still has a high degree of anxiety about the seemingly endless conflicts between her work life and her personal life. She wishes she could find more balance, meaning, purpose, and even spirituality through her work. She has become very advanced in terms of using the tools of information technology but she sometimes pauses to wonder about the meaning of it all.

Most of all, Alica is indeed a very independent person, one who has a special capacity to lead herself. The technology is forcing a critical reevaluation of how we go about doing our work.

The Organization of the 21st Century

This is a book about leadership for the organization of the 21st century. There's no question that our world has become very complicated and that it is changing at an unprecedented rate. Unfortunately, many of our management practices have not kept up with these changes. One of the greatest opportunities for change and advancement centers on the meaningful mobilization of human effort and innovative behavior through contemporary organizations. Many of these new forms of organizing cry out for innovative ways of leading and organizing people at work. The potential payoffs are immense. Information and knowledge work is transforming organizational processes. Here are some changes we can expect to see:[3]

▶ By 2005, 75 percent of global enterprises will require major overhauls of people management, workplace policies and workforce planning in response to a shift to knowledge as the center of wealth production.

- The impact is on the workplace—the people and how they work—and the focus is on knowledge as the primary source of capability and competitive advantage.

- Efforts to Internet-enable employees represent initial steps in fueling profound cultural change. This will impact not only the manner in which such enterprises act as suppliers and customers in the world of e-business, but also the character of their workforce and their workplaces.

- Enterprises in North America spend an average of 2.9 percent of revenue on technology, which is an average of $7,756 annually for each employee.

Since our own experience relates primarily to business organizations, they will generally be the focus of our discussion. We believe, however, that these fundamental challenges stretch to nearly all aspects of our lives—our relationships, the way we raise our children, the educational process, and so forth. The business organization is clearly moving from an industrial enterprise model toward a knowledge-based enterprise model. The table on the following page shows some of the differences between these two perspectives.[4]

How is organizational structure changing to reflect the technological revolution? The baseline for comparison is the old vertical pyramid, with its emphasis on hierarchical command and control. For example, in the 1960s one new recruit to the management ranks of Ford Motor Company traced the actual chain of command from himself to the CEO, Henry Ford II. He found a total of 13 levels—that is, a chain of 11 "bosses"—between himself and Ford.

Several forms of organizational structure have emerged as more appropriate for the 21st century. Probably the first type that comes to mind for most is the horizontal organization, with a flat structure, large spans of control, and short chains of command. A second type is the pure project-based organization; that is, work is accomplished through transitory teams, each of which has a finite beginning and end. The life of an employee in this organization is a series of memberships from one team to another. Career advancement in

The Industrial Enterprise	The Knowledge-Based Enterprise
Corporate Attributes	**Corporate Attributes**
‣ Economics of scale	‣ Smaller business units
‣ Standardization of work	‣ Customization of work
‣ Standardization of workforce	‣ Flexible, skill based work-force
‣ Financial capital as scarce resource	‣ Human capital as a scarce resource
‣ Corporate HQ as operational controller	‣ Corporate HQ as advisor & core competency guardian
‣ Hierarchical pyramid structure	‣ Flat or networked structure
‣ Employees seen as expense	‣ Employees seen as investment
‣ Internally focused top-down governance	‣ Both internal and external distributed governance
‣ Individualistic orientation	‣ Team orientation
‣ Information based on "need to know"	‣ Open & distributed information system
‣ Vertical decision making	‣ Distributed decision making
‣ Emphasis on stability	‣ Emphasis on change
‣ Emphasis on vertical leader-ship	‣ Emphasis on empowered self-leadership

Source: *Visions of the Future*: Flowchart Report from the Corporate Leadership Council, Washington, D.C.

these types of structures takes on a whole new meaning—it's hard to "climb the ladder" when there are very few rungs.

Another structural form is the networked organization, or a type of consortium or alliance of legal entities, each of which depends on the other to exist. In today's world of manufacturing high-tech products, for example, very few companies now elect to go the route of true vertical integration. Instead, partnerships are forged through networks, joint ventures, and integrated supply chains. The glue that makes all of this possible is the "b2b" (Internet-based business-to-business) communication network, where information flows through the Internet (or an Intranet) in a speedy and timely fashion.

For most of these newer organizational forms, teams are the norm rather than the exception. There are many different kinds of teams: concurrent engineering teams, product or quality improvement teams, product launch teams, focused task forces, self-directed teams, top management teams, and so on. A critical feature of these teams is that they are invested with a significant degree of empowerment, or decision-making authority. (More about teams in a later chapter.)

PEOPLE OF THE INFORMATION REVOLUTION

These new organizational structures are typically run by people who demand a different kind of culture than the old command-and-control format. Today, people are better educated and demand more from their jobs than a paycheck. Frequently, employees are more committed to their profession than to their company. This means that most people won't stand for being closely managed and directed anymore, and they would probably be wasting their unique talents and capabilities if they did. Over a decade ago, in his prescient book *The Gold-Collar Worker*, Robert E. Kelley emphasized the deeper significance of the emergence of the younger, upscale, educated work force. He discussed a "new breed of workers" and called for business to adapt to their special characteristics.[5]

Truly valued employees will be valued not so much for their hierarchical position, what they do, or even for what they know, which is the traditional definition of a knowledge worker. Instead, the most valued employees will be characterized by a keen capacity to learn, or what they are capable of knowing quickly.

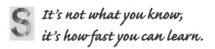

It's not what you know,
it's how fast you can learn.

Knowledge and learning will become the differentiating assets of the 21st century. Employees will know how to quickly access information, and more importantly how to filter, evaluate, summarize, and condense information into an action plan. They will possess a high degree of flexibility and adaptability in keeping up with the ever-advancing technology, yet will be increasingly adroit at dealing with people. They will not see their career as climbing a hierarchical ladder in a single company but will have a strong sense of mobility and will be highly motivated by moving from challenge to challenge. Self-fulfillment will replace corporate loyalty as a dominant value. They will not be uncomfortable with periods of self-employment or even unemployment, and will occasionally take a hiatus for educational renewal.

LEADERSHIP FOR THE 21ST CENTURY

Empowerment is the key word—the oil that lubricates the exercise of knowledge. According to Jack Welch, the organization of the 21st century will concentrate on the objective of assuring that each person has the information and authority they need to make decisions.

There will be many ways of doing things right, not just one right way. Both individuals and teams will be empowered, but this empowerment will represent something more advanced than the buzzword usually implies today. People will be empowered to be true self-leaders, and will increasingly possess the capability to handle this vast increase in authority.

We find ourselves today on the cutting edge of a chain of causation. The technological revolution is causing a change in the ways organizations structure themselves. The changes in structure require rather radical changes in the culture—the social systems within these organizations. The essence of this cultural change is the investment in and emphasis on knowledge work, the way people process and transform information. This emerging culture places high value on mentorship, learning, initiative and creativity. To be truly effective, the knowledge worker needs to be empowered at an advanced level. Talented and empowered human capital will become the prime ingredient of organizational success. Most of all, people need to be able to lead themselves.

The future is coming so fast, we can't possibly predict it; we can only learn to respond quickly.

—Steven Kerr[6]

This brings us full circle, back to the primary leadership challenge. How can a leader develop the self-leadership needed to run the organization of the 21st century? The old model of the charismatic lone star will be gone. Later in the book, we spell out this new mode of leadership—SuperLeadership—starting with ideas for how to lead individuals to be self-leaders, moving on to the ideas for leading teams to be self-led, and then suggesting ideas for developing a total culture of self-leadership throughout an organization.

First, however, let's cover a few fundamental ideas about how a leader can lead others to lead themselves.

WHAT IS SELF-LEADERSHIP AND SUPERLEADERSHIP?

Over the past twenty years, through our consulting, research, and writing, we have developed a set of ideas that we believe can help meet the challenge of leading in the 21st century. We use the labels of *self-leadership* and *SuperLeadership* to characterize a different approach to leadership. Since these terms are the keystone of our ideas, it's worthwhile to briefly define them.

Self-leadership is an extensive set of strategies focused on the behaviors, thoughts, and feelings that we use to exert influence over ourselves. Self-leadership is what people do to lead themselves. In some ways, self-leadership might also be thought of as a form of advanced followership or, perhaps more accurately, leadership focused on oneself that enables a redefining of traditional followership. That is, if they are given the autonomy and responsibility to control their own lives, what *specifically* can followers who are becoming self-leaders do to meet this challenge in a responsible way?

We have heard the employee who complains, "They say they want us to be empowered around here. As of today, I'm supposed to be 'empowered.' I don't understand what that means. What am I supposed to do that's different?" In answer, self-leadership provides a set of guidelines for how an employee can responsibly meet the challenge of so-called empowerment.

 Self-leadership is focused on the behaviors and thoughts that people use to influence themselves.

Developing each person into an effective self-leader is a formidable yet fascinating challenge. The leader who does this is called a *SuperLeader*, a term that applies to the manager and executive who has responsibility for leading others, especially their direct-report employees.

More specifically, a SuperLeader is one who leads others to lead themselves. The SuperLeader designs and implements the system that allows and teaches employees to be self-leaders. The approach consists of an extensive set of behaviors, all intended to provide so-called followers with the behavioral and cognitive skills necessary to exercise self-leadership. The SuperLeader asks, "What can I do to lead others to lead themselves?"

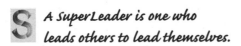 *A SuperLeader is one who leads others to lead themselves.*

In the pages that follow, we will develop these ideas in some detail. We will present the behavior and thought-focused strategies that are the essence of self-leadership—understanding self-leadership is a critical first step to understanding SuperLeadership. And we will especially focus on the skills that form the basis for Super-Leadership. We hope these ideas will not be seen as a panacea—they're not—but as a carefully designed game plan intended to capitalize on the long-term potential of each person.

Employee Self-Leadership Is the Key to 21st Century Leadership

We propose a fundamentally different approach to leading people that will become increasingly important as we move further into the 21st century. We refer to this approach as *SuperLeadership: leading others to lead themselves*. Our ideas are rooted in the view that essentially all control over employees is *ultimately* self-imposed. Regardless of where controls come from (for example, from a manager or a company policy), the effect they have depends on how these controls are evaluated, accepted, and translated by each employee into his or her own personal commitment.

Just as organizations provide their members with standards, evaluations, rewards, and corrective feedback, individuals provide and experience these same basic elements from within. Employees have expectations regarding their own performance, and react positively or negatively toward themselves in response to their own self-evaluations.

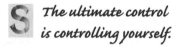

S *The ultimate control is controlling yourself.*

This is a most important point to make. Typically, organizational attempts at employee control do not recognize the important role of the person's "self." Organizational standards will not significantly influence employee behavior if they are not accepted. Similarly, organizational rewards will have a limited effect in producing behavior that is controlled from within. Regardless of how employee performance is appraised, the performance evaluations that will carry the most weight will be the evaluations that employees make of themselves.

We believe the principal means of establishing the commitment and enthusiasm necessary to achieve true long-term excellence in an organization is to unleash the self-leadership potential within each person. Tight external control that undermines or displaces an employee's self-control system may produce compliance. Commitment to excellence, however, flows from the powerful leadership potential within.

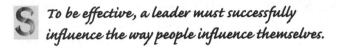

To be effective, a leader must successfully influence the way people influence themselves.

Over-reliance on external control can produce some very dysfunctional outcomes. External control can result in bureaucratic behavior in which people focus their efforts only on what is measured and rewarded by the organization, neglecting many other important activities. It can also lead to other dysfunctional behaviors and outcomes, such as the feeding of management information systems with inaccurate data that artificially enhances individual performance standings, compliance rather than commitment, and a number of other problems.

A rigid performance appraisal system for salespeople that focuses on established sales procedures and standards may be effective in producing short-term sales increases, for example. But long-term performance can suffer because of a lack of attention to servicing existing clients. Moreover, this external control process can interfere with the unique creativity and interests an employee needs to express in order to become committed to the job.

An overemphasis on external rewards at the expense of internal (or natural) rewards can undermine important aspects of individual motivation. If the emphasis is placed on what people will *get* for doing their work (money, promotions, and so on) rather than on the positive aspects of doing the task itself—the natural enjoyment of a job well done—then, we would argue, meaningful commitment to high achievement is at risk. This suggests that the way control and leadership are viewed is all too often very limited. We propose a new viewpoint for leadership as we look ahead to the coming decades—one that utilizes the unique self-leadership capability within each person.

SuperLeadership Versus
Traditional Views of Leadership

SuperLeadership is fundamentally different from traditional views of leadership. In the next chapter we review these differences in detail The main objective of SuperLeadership is to stimulate and facilitate self-leadership capability and practice and, further, to make the self-leadership process the central target of external influence. Self-leadership is viewed as a powerful opportunity for achieving high performance rather than as a threat to external control and authority. In fact, if leaders really want followers to develop into high performers, providing them with the autonomy and responsibility to be more in charge of themselves and their work is essential.

The top-down, hard-nosed autocrat will become an artifact of history, replaced by leaders who are obsessed with the development of their followers.

In our research we have observed striking examples of employee self-leadership when companies implement new forms of "team" organization. In work systems using self-managing teams, we saw the workers themselves make many work-related decisions such as assignments to equipment, the handling of quality and personnel problems, adjustments to work-shift scheduling, budget recommendations, and many other concerns that have traditionally been the responsibility of management. We also noticed employees talking about "our business," actively striving to eliminate quality problems and to increase productivity, solving technical problems, and, most of all, working *with* not *against* management to make "their company" more profitable. Workers even did what traditionally have been viewed as "crazy" things like staying after a shift was over to lend a hand if it was needed and dropping in on weekends, without pay, to make sure the equipment was shut down properly.

Most of all, these employees seemed to believe in and be committed to their work to a degree we had not previously thought possible. More and more these evolved management practices that originally emerged in manufacturing systems, especially the use of empowered teams, have swept across service- and knowledge-based work settings.

Interestingly, as we look to the future of the information-based organizations of the 21st century, our best model of leadership may derive from experiences in manufacturing, where team-oriented SuperLeadership has shown significant increases in effectiveness and productivity. Attempts to force people into some externally designed mold not only undermine individual potential, but are likely to deprive an organization of its long-term opportunity to achieve high performance. The 21st-century leader should strive to unleash the full talents of people by stimulating their own capability for self-leadership.

The unleashing of self-leadership is a very different way of viewing the process of leadership and control. Such an approach, however, is not entirely new in practice. In fact, several trends are apparent that suggest that such changes have been under way for some time. For example, almost two decades ago, in his best-selling book *Megatrends*, John Naisbitt identified several future trends that are very consistent with an increased emphasis on self-control.[7] Four of the ten trends he identified were moves from centralization to decentralization, from institutional help to self-help, from representative democracy to participative democracy, and from hierarchies to networking. These trends, now clearly under way, represent a move away from more formalized structures and institutions toward greater diversity and an emphasis on grass roots in our society. Most of all, they suggest a recognition of people as individuals and as uniquely valuable resources.

S SuperLeadership is about a fundamentally different approach that stimulates and facilitates self-leadership in others . . . that recognizes self-influence as a powerful opportunity for achieving excellence rather than as a threat to authority.

As highlighted in the beginning of this chapter, the increase of people working autonomously in their homes (telecommuters) with the aid of fax machines, home computers, the Internet, PC-based videoconferencing, and other technological tools, has created a significant trend toward increased reliance on self-leadership in organizational practice. How do we provide leadership to people who are located in remote places? In addition, many organizations—frequently the better performing ones—have been increasingly emphasizing empowerment and various forms of autonomy as a means of increasing the capability and performance of their workforce.

D. Quinn Mills, a professor at Harvard Business School, discussed the consequences of traditional leadership on a corps of younger middle managers.[8] When a new CEO issued his edict about the objectives of the company, Mills discusses how an observer could see ". . . the lights go out in many eyes. The same managers in whom [the CEO] had once sensed a seemingly genuine desire to have a bigger, better company suddenly appeared disaffected and sullen. Even when [the CEO] announced the chance of hefty bonuses . . . enthusiasm among the assembled managers was conspicuous by its absence."

Mills further described the longer-term consequences of this action: "Within a year, several of the company's best managers had quit. Competitors were still gaining on the company, yet morale was so low that no one was pushing to turn the situation around." This CEO was no SuperLeader! He had forgotten the importance of gaining the commitment of younger managers as a critical step on the road to success.

> *The time is ripe for a new perspective on leadership. . . . SuperLeadership—leading others to lead themselves—can help meet this challenge.*

We are very optimistic about our economic future because we realize that we have barely scratched the surface of our most powerful resource for economic and social progress—the vast potential for self-discovery within each person. The tremendous power of committed, motivated, self-led people can be the key to economic and social progress beyond what our world has ever seen.

Traditional control methods will not allow this potential to be unleashed. For years, too many organizations have experienced employee compliance rather than commitment, mediocre productivity and quality, and dissatisfaction among their workforce. Increases in globalization and international competition have made it all too apparent that such traditional controls can no longer be tolerated if companies are to survive and maintain their world standing. Achieving the ideal of commitment to high performance calls for a new era of facilitating the internal energy and potential of people through widespread self-leadership. Striving to meet this challenge through SuperLeadership is at the heart of this important quest.

The Challenge and Opportunity of Leading in the New Era

As we move further into the new century and the new millennium, we believe this is a great time to be in business. Employee productivity and product quality have risen significantly in the last few years and American business has reemerged as a world leader. Opportunities for achieving great things and for experiencing fulfillment in work and life have never been greater. Medical advances and increased standards of living have enabled people to enjoy longer and healthier lives. Educational opportunities are fantastic, and the war on ignorance has had many victories—preschool, primary school, colleges and universities, continuing and adult education, home computers, the Internet . . . the tally is impressive. And scientific advances have provided many impressive technologies, such as automated factories, robotics, palm computers, biotechnology, advanced information systems, and so on, which only a few decades ago would have seemed impossible. If we take stock of the positive opportunities that exist for corporations and their employees, it is difficult to be blind to the potential.

But the challenges, obviously, are great. It's highly unlikely that people can reasonably expect to learn everything they'll need to be successful in their careers during "school years." It's no longer what you know, but knowing how to learn. Lifelong learning is no longer a luxury; it's now a requirement for survival. Most people cannot possess all the knowledge required to perform their work. If we truly aspire to high performance, we need to be continually learning and benefiting from the knowledge of others.

The 21st century has brought many challenges and many opportunities. Self-leadership is the key to enhancing the learning that is necessary to enable us to meet the challenges of this information-rich and knowledge-based era. And SuperLeadership provides the tools for leaders to be able to create this self-leadership in others.

Dennis Bakke of AES Corporation

Ken A. Smith

Dennis Bakke, cofounder and CEO of AES Corporation, is widely considered to be among today's most successful corporate leaders. Together with Roger Sant, Bakke founded AES as an international independent power company in 1981 with the mission to serve the world's need for electricity by offering clean, safe, and reliable power in a socially responsible way.

While the operating and financial performance of AES has been remarkable, Bakke would argue that his greater success lies in the people of AES. *Harvard Business Review*, *Fast Company*, *Business Week*, and others have called Bakke one of the most "enlightened" corporate leaders of the modern era, a role model for those who are committed to developing and empowering others. We call him a "SuperLeader."

FROM PERSONAL TO CORPORATE VALUES

Bakke is a SuperLeader whose leadership is rooted in two primary beliefs that predate the founding of AES. First, he believes that businesses do not exist primarily to make money; they exist to serve. Says Bakke, "The purpose of business and the purpose of AES [is] stewarding resources in order to meet a need in society. You start with that premise. If you don't start with that premise, none of this stuff makes sense."[1]

Second, people matter. They have desires and skills that can and should be developed. So, says Bakke, "People development is almost as high a purpose as meeting a need in society."

THE PERFORMANCE OF AES

AES currently has operations in 24 countries with 146 power plants in operation or under construction, yielding a combined capacity of 52,000 megawatts of electricity. The distribution business, which represents 39 percent of revenues, sells electricity to approximately 15 million consumers around the world including commercial, industrial, governmental and residential customers. Capitalizing on recent moves toward privatization and deregulation of electric utilities, in 1999 AES had a portfolio of 165 active new business ideas in over 50 countries.

AES has pursued a strategy of operating excellence, resulting in high standards of operation and leadership in environmental matters associated with independent power production. On average, AES operates its worldwide power plants at 60 percent of the permitted U.S. emission levels, thereby exceeding the federal performance standards mandated for such plants under the Clean Air Act. AES has also offset carbon dioxide emissions by funding projects such as the planting of trees in Guatemala and the preservation of forest land in Paraguay. In 1999, AES voluntarily made a risky $32 million investment to develop the largest selective catalytic reduction reactor ever built on a coal-fired boiler, which reduced nitrogen oxides (NOx) emissions in its New York plant by 90 percent. AES has also established a better-than-average safety record in its industry.

AES went public in 1991 and is now included in the S&P 500. In 1999, the company generated $3.3 billion in revenues on $21 billion in assets. By early 2000, its market value reached $17.7 billion. The company has ranked on *Fortune*'s list of America's 100 fastest-growing companies. By any standard, Bakke has created a successful business enterprise.

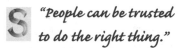

"*People can be trusted
to do the right thing.*"

Bakke is articulate about the connection between this philosophy and his deeply held spiritual beliefs. He believes that people are spiritual beings with inherent, individual worth. People are special and unique; they are creative, accountable, and trustworthy. But Bakke also recognizes that people are fallible, so forgiveness and reconciliation are necessary dimensions of human interaction. Thus, Bakke desires to engage the whole person in the business enterprise and treat mistakes as learning opportunities. AES's nonhierarchical structure clearly reflects this.

Finally, Bakke believes that stewardship of the earth and its resources for the benefit of all is a primary responsibility of mankind. The company's commitment to social responsibility is a logical result.

Bakke's commitment to the value of people also derives from his experience of strong personal relationships between members of AES's founding team, which predate the founding of the company. Bakke worked as Roger Sant's deputy at the Federal Energy Administration from 1974 to 1976, and then at the Energy Productivity Center at Carnegie-Mellon University from 1977 to 1981. Sant then served as AES's founding CEO, with Bakke filling the roles of president and chief operating officer. During these years Bakke observed Sant's commitment to developing those around him, and personally benefited from Sant's mentoring. The experience led Bakke to the conclusion that relationships are key to fostering individual growth; they are fundamental to effective SuperLeadership. Says Bakke, "Our goal was to build a company that we ourselves would want to work in."

Bakke's personal philosophy is clearly reflected in AES's four core values, which are:

- To act with integrity

- To be fair

- To have fun

- To be socially responsible

Bakke is quick to point out that these are "shared" values, originally articulated by the founders and officers; they are not exclusively his own creation. Nevertheless, he views his primary role as CEO and leader to be communicating and holding the company to these values. Says Bakke, "The only thing that we hold tightly as to what has to be done are the four values."

Bakke describes *integrity* as " ... it fits together as a whole ... wholeness, completeness." In practice this means that the things AES people say and do in all parts of the company should fit together with truth and consistency. "The main thing we do is ask the question, 'What did we commit?'" Bakke explains. "We have a rule here that says, 'Whoever is the senior person at any meeting'—I don't care if you've been here one day or ten years—'can commit the company.' That's almost unheard of, because nobody is ever given authority to commit their company ... unless you're at the CEO level, and sometimes I'm not so sure about that." But at AES, people engaged in negotiation can commit the company, and they know the company will back them up.

Fairness means treating its people, customers, suppliers, stockholders, governments, and the communities in which AES operates fairly. Defining what is fair is often difficult, but the main point is that the company believes it is helpful to question routinely the relative fairness of alternative courses of action. This means that AES does not try to get the most out of each negotiation or transaction to the detriment of others. Bakke challenges his people to ask, "Is it fair? Would I feel as good on the other side of the table as I feel on this side of the table about the outcome of this meeting, or this decision, with my employee or supervisor or customer?"

The third value is *fun.* "If it isn't fun we don't want it," says Bakke. "We either want to quit or change something that we're doing." Bakke wants the people AES employs, and those with whom the company interacts, to have fun in their work. He elaborates: "By fun we don't mean party fun. We're talking about creating an environment where people can use their gifts and skills productively to help meet a need in society and thereby enjoy the time spent at AES." What is "fun" is that people are fully engaged. "It's that creative environment where people can thrive and become stars.... It's where you're trying to make other people stars," says Bakke. "We can break down the barriers so folks can use those wonderful gifts and skills that they've been given or acquired along the way. That's what people really find fun. And that's what we're trying to do."

The fourth value is *social responsibility.* "We see ourselves as a citizen of the world," says Bakke. This value presumes that AES has a responsibility to be involved in projects that provide social benefits, such as lower costs to customers, a high degree of safety and reliability, increased employment, and a cleaner environment. "We try to do things that you'd like your neighbor to do."

MODELING AND ENCOURAGING SUPERLEADERSHIP

AES's values, and Dennis Bakke's personal leadership, focus on people. Whether being responsive to needs of people outside the company (e.g., social responsibility) or AES's own (e.g., fun), the focus is on giving people the opportunity to develop and lead themselves.

Modeling Self-Leadership

An important aspect of Bakke's leadership is modeling self-leadership behaviors for the organization. One process through which this is done has been annual visits to the plants by the corporation's top executives. "Every officer has to go once a year to one plant for a week," says Bakke. "It's partly symbolic, partly it's a tremendous time to get to know some of the folks." An important part of the symbolism is that senior managers interact with employees in a way that demonstrates their similar values and oneness of purpose.

It was during his early plant visits that Bakke observed that people throughout the company have the same motivations and the same concerns. So Bakke asked, "Why are [people in the plants] being managed in a different way from what we do in Arlington? Why are the maintenance people all here in their own group, and office people in another? And here are operators, and the operators can't do any maintenance? Maintenance people have to come and do these kinds of things? It's the old union thing, where you hold the plug and I'll plug it in. I said, 'Why do we do that?'"

Bakke elaborates, "One guy was complaining, 'Well, you know, maintenance guys never do this. They never get it done. I put the work order in and it never gets done. And *they* wouldn't let *us* do it. And *they* . . .' I started asking, 'Well, who in the world are "They?"' 'Well, uh . . . the guys in Arlington,' or 'the people in the administration building,' or 'the plant manager.' People very seldom could tell you who 'they' were, but it was somebody out there. *Somebody* other than themselves was responsible for their job and making them helpless."

So AES came up with an "Anti-They" campaign to communicate the kind of self-responsible behavior the company needed. "Everyone had a great time with it," says Bakke. "Anti-They. The big international symbol, 'They' with a line through it. . . . A guy in the control room would say, 'Well, *they* won't. *They* don't care. *They* don't want to do this.' We'd say, 'Who's *they*?' Now they do it to each other, trying to get people to say *we*."

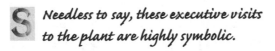

Needless to say, these executive visits to the plant are highly symbolic.

The campaign against "they" is one outgrowth of the annual visit to plants by senior managers. Each executive voluntarily spends at least one week at a specific operating plant—not to review or receive briefings, but to participate in the everyday activities of the plant by carrying out the work assigned to a specific job. Each executive takes on at least one job per day, and some of these jobs can be fairly rough or dirty. The impact of these visits is significant. It conveys the notion that each job is important, and that no one is too good to work at any job—no matter how rough or dirty it is. It also evokes a strong sense of loyalty, commitment, and a sense of ownership throughout the company. In addition to membership in their immediate work team, each employee feels a part of the larger organizational team. And knowing where one fits in is fundamental to being able to lead oneself.

Fostering Self-Leadership

To foster self-leadership, Bakke has sought to move AES employees from hourly wages to salaried positions. By 1998, 50 percent of AES employees were salaried, but Bakke is working toward the day when there won't be any hourly workers anywhere in the world. According to Bakke, "When you pay someone a salary and make them eligible for bonuses and stock ownership, you are saying, 'Our assumptions about you are no different from those we have about the plant leader. You can and should bring your brainpower and soul—your whole person—to work.'"[2] In effect the company is saying, "You are a part of this organization; you have the same worth as everyone else."

Bakke also desires that people take responsibility for their own career development. One way to do this is to provide opportunities for job rotation. Bakke recalls: "The example of Pete Norgeot's career with us is a good case in point. Before joining our Thames plant in Connecticut, he was a heavy-machine operator. His first assignment with us was as a member of the fuel-handling team. He stayed with that team for six months, then shifted to the water treatment team, and then to the boiler team. For three years, he basically went from group to group. He studied all the technical books he could—we have manuals on every aspect of our operation, and you can use them to help prepare for the qualification exams that you must pass before you can work in an area. After spending three years at Thames, he learned of an opportunity in our Medway plant in England, and he took it. After a few years, he was selected to be the plant manager at our new Barry facility in Wales."[3]

The idea of taking responsibility for your own career, making the effort to develop yourself and being compensated accordingly, is consistent with AES's definition of "fun" as a value. Treating employees as salaried professionals and providing them opportunities for development are but two of the ways Bakke seeks to foster self-management.

Summary

Thus far we have seen that Dennis Bakke, as a SuperLeader, personally models self-leadership and fosters self-leadership in others. His motivation comes from the personal philosophy that businesses exist to meet a need in society, and that people are valuable and should be developed. This philosophy has in turn given rise to a set of shared company values that delineate how AES conducts its business.

Leadership requires that one be clear on direction and be able to motivate others to its pursuit. SuperLeadership, however, requires transfer of ownership of direction and motivation to those engaged in the pursuit, such that they lead themselves. For Bakke, AES's shared values are a primary mechanism for this transfer of ownership. Later in the book we will revisit Dennis Bakke and AES Corporation to review other aspects of SuperLeadership in action.

2 The Strongman, Transactor, Visionary Hero, and SuperLeader

GENERAL **D**WIGHT **D. E**ISENHOWER had a high opinion of the potential of the common man.[1] In 1967 he wrote: "In our Army, it was thought that every private had at least a second lieutenant's gold bars somewhere in him and he was helped and encouraged to earn them. . . . I am inclined by nature to be optimistic about the capacity of a person to rise higher than he or she has thought possible, once interest and ambition are aroused."[2]

Since he thought well of others, he intuitively understood the advantage of sharing information with subordinates. For example, he wrote that "The Army . . . as far back as the days of von Steuben, learned that Americans either will not or cannot fight at maximum efficiency unless they understand the why and wherefore of their orders."[3]

Baron Friedrich von Steuben, a Prussian-born American general during the Revolutionary War, found that American soldiers required something special to fight at maximum efficiency. In other words, these soldiers required leadership that matched their personal goals to reach the targets of the army. To that end, von Steuben modified his own European-based command practices, trying to understand the individual American soldier's role and motivation.

This optimistic viewpoint of man-in-general is a fairly common characteristic of SuperLeaders. They seem to have unlimited faith that, if given the opportunity to perform, most people will come through.

What is *your* viewpoint of the "common man"? How do you think your followers are likely to react if given the opportunity for independent responsibility? How much time and effort do you spend preparing your followers for self-leadership? The way you answer these questions is likely to be very strongly predictive of your own leadership. Can you prepare your followers to work in a creative and independent mode?

Whenever we think of leadership, we typically think of some category or type of leader. Often we call this "leadership style." What we are usually talking about is a pattern of behaviors that together we can think of as "style" or "type." The previous story of Dwight Eisenhower represents a combination of types. Of course we think of him as a Visionary Hero type, but we also think of him as a Super-Leader.

In this chapter we define four prominent types of leaders: the Strongman, the Transactor, the Visionary Hero, and the Super-Leader. One purpose of this discussion is to ask yourself the question: "What type of leader am I?" And further, "What type of leader do I want to be?"

WHAT IS LEADERSHIP?

There is an old Norse word, *Laed*, meaning "to determine the *course* of a ship." Our modern word "to lead" clearly is derived from this ancient Viking expression. And it's easy to think of the CEO of our contemporary organization as one who determines the *course* of the ship or, in this case, organization. But in the business environment of the 21st century, how should this guidance take place? Today we describe many organizations as consisting of clusters and flows of "knowledge" and "information" and as being staffed by "knowledge workers." This introduces a challenging question for leadership: What kind of leader do we need in order to create and lead the knowledge workers of the 21st century?

Clearly, the word *leadership* itself is value-laden. We usually think of the word in positive terms, one who has a special capacity. Most of us would rather be a "leader" than a "manager," or a "leader" rather than a "politician." Sometimes the word *leadership* refers to a role rather than behaviors. We recently heard an executive from Xerox, for example, refer to the Xerox managers as "the leadership." Personally, we are not comfortable with this definition because it implies that those in the lower ranks are *not* leaders—and in fact, this book is about the diffusion of leadership throughout an organization, not just at the top. Some of the most remarkable leaders of all time have not had the benefit of formal position to support their leadership.

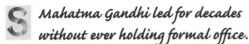 *Mahatma Gandhi led for decades without ever holding formal office.*

There are hundreds of definitions of leadership. But to us, fundamentally leadership means influence—the influence of people. This is a broad definition, and would include a wide variety of behaviors intended to influence others. In this chapter we briefly define and discuss various ways of influencing others—that is, different types or "styles" of leadership. Later throughout the book we focus mainly on SuperLeadership, a particular kind of empowering leadership that concentrates on leading others to lead themselves.

Most leadership perspectives view the leader as the only source of influence. The leader leads (influences) and followers follow (are influenced). This leader-centric view of influence was adequate for hundreds of years but, especially recently, many limitations of this view have emerged. In the 21st century the challenge of influence has indeed passed over a new threshold that views leadership in a whole new light. In this chapter we trace some of the primary types of influence that have defined most leadership practice for several decades, and even centuries. Each of the types we discuss is still alive and well in many settings, and each still has a place in the leader's repertoire. Yet, all too often, poor choices are made regarding which leadership types are used in specific situations and which are emphasized the most overall.

In the past, especially in our book *Company of Heroes*, we used the terms Strongman, Transactor, Visionary Hero, and SuperLeader to identify different leader types. Here we continue with these labels that capture the spirit of the primary types of leadership each of us can understand and identify.

THE STRONGMAN

Sometimes when we think of leadership, the rough-and-tough image of John Wayne comes to mind. He is not afraid to knock some heads to get followers to do what he wants them to do. We see a figure larger than life, who leads by commanding others. We can also think of this leader as the "Boss." He uses the authority of his position to influence others, who mainly comply out of fear. If the job is not performed as commanded, some significant form of punishment is delivered to the guilty party. The most common behaviors of this leader are instruction, command, assigned goals, threat, intimidation, and reprimand.

Roberto Goizueta's 16-year tenure as CEO of Atlanta-based Coca-Cola was a hard act to follow. Goizueta was highly regarded as a charismatic Visionary Hero, whose flamboyant style characterized his remarkable leadership. Coke's value had increased from $4.3 billion to $147 billion[4] before his untimely death. But the board was confident when it appointed Doug Ivester as Goizueta's successor. After all, Ivester had been groomed by Goizueta over several years.

But Ivester lasted only two years. With earnings declines in both years, the board found it necessary to move on to a new CEO. According to *Fortune* magazine, the problem was not Ivester's experience or intellectual capacity but a failure of "that ethereal thing called leadership."

Ivester was known for his grasp of the tiniest detail. He seemed to be obsessed with doing things in an orderly, rational way. "He took pride in being a substance-over-style guy.... And while he was in command of a vast number of details, he seemed to lose sight of the big picture." Ivester was high on discipline and control, telling *Fortune*, "We operate with a rigid control system." While he invested significantly in developing technology for a modern data-driven information system, the information contributed to his isolation. The vision that Goizueta had established over the years seemed to have become lost.

To us, Ivester is an example of a Strongman type of leader. He was highly directive and intolerant of deviations from the prescribed way of doing things. Most of all he seemed unaware of the image, and encouragement of initiative and creativity, that are necessary with a market-driven company like Coke. While Strongman leadership may create a response in the short term, the longer-term effects can be quite devastating, especially when creativity is a necessary element for success.

THE TRANSACTOR

The second view of leadership is the Transactor, who enters into an exchange relationship with others. This leader type may trigger memories of pigeons pecking at levers in order to get food pellet rewards during experiments that were part of the behavior modification movement in the 1960s and 1970s, with its emphasis on positive reinforcement principles. This leader influences through the dispensation of rewards in exchange for compliance from followers. The behaviors most frequently used by this leader are personal and material rewards that are given in return for effort, performance, and loyalty to the leader.

Followers of the Transactor take a calculative view of their work: "I will do what he/she wants as long as the rewards keep coming." Transactor leadership is a classic, time-honored type of leadership found in the corporate world. Transactor leadership is still widely practiced today and, combined with some Visionary Hero leadership and a bit of Strongman leadership, can still be effective within the short term. Consider the case of Lawrence J. Ellison, chairman of number-two software maker Oracle Corporation:[5]

Oracle Corporation, with its market position in database software, has become a leading power in applying database software to the Internet revolution. According to *Business Week* magazine, CEO Lawrence Ellison has developed a system of leadership that he believes is critical in leading the company into the 21st century. The key to Ellison's philosophy is the use of Internet and database technology to construct an organization that can be characterized as "centralized control."

Ellison is clearly a Visionary Hero type of leader, as demonstrated by his aggressive mission of transforming Oracle from a database-specialized company into an Internet and b2b powerhouse. But Ellison also tends to favor Transactor methods to implement this changeover. Ellison has transformed Oracle into a tightly run company. "Larry has the people in this company screwed down tight," says chief financial officer Jeffrey O. Henley.

Ellison personally rewrote sales contracts and developed pricing standards to reduce the control and flexibility of the field salespeople. According to Ellison, "All the individuality is bled out of the system and replaced by standards. People don't run their own show anymore."

The sales reps are paid well, but under tight control. According to *Business Week*, "Ellison's approach is to use the carrot first, and then the stick." Ellison's main objective is to boost the profit margins, not sales goals, and he compensates his country managers well for meeting ambitious profit-margin targets.

Ellison's leadership even intrudes into the work territory of some of his closest sidekicks. Oracle president Raymond J. Lane recounts the story of Ellison inserting himself into Lane's consulting and sales responsibilities. "All of a sudden, Larry is in your mess kit drilling down for four hours. . . . Some days I'll walk out of a meeting saying, 'I don't need this.'" But Lane doesn't really seem to object. He's quite happy with the bottom line results: "What Larry's doing is working . . . look at the stock price."

Certainly, at certain times and places, Transactor leadership has its merits. We think of President Lyndon Johnson, for example, who was the consummate Transactor leader in his successful attempts to guide Congress through the civil rights legislation of the mid-1960s.

THE VISIONARY HERO

The most popular current view of leadership is the exciting and charismatic leader who inspires and motivates others. We call this type the Visionary Hero. This type is characterized by an ability to create a highly motivating and absorbing vision of the future. This leader has the capacity to energize others to pursue the vision. For many, this leader is almost larger than life and sometimes attains a mythic reputation.

> *"... In a crisis, we tend to look for the wrong kind of leadership. ... We should be calling for leadership that will challenge us to face problems for which there are no simple, painless solutions— problems that require us to learn new ways."*
>
> —Ronald A. Heifetz[6]

While many view this type of leadership very positively in terms of inspiring others to pursue a captivating cause, we sometimes forget that Visionary Hero leadership is mainly a top-down influence process. The leader is the primary source of wisdom and direction, and tends to occupy the spotlight while followers fade into the shadows. The leader's power is based on a capability to generate a commitment by the follower to the leader's vision and persona. The leader uses behaviors such as formulating and communicating a vision, exhortation, inspiration and persuasion, and challenge to the status quo. Other terms that have been used to describe this leader are "transformational" and "charismatic." Consider the case of Richard Branson, one of the most remarkable Visionary Hero leaders of our time:[7]

Richard Branson is the founder and CEO of the Virgin Group, one of the world's most prominent global brands. Their business holdings include a wide variety of products and services, of which Virgin Atlantic Airlines is perhaps the most prominent. Branson is viewed by the public as a celebrity, entrepreneur, adventurer and risk-taker. These viewpoints are pivotal in interpreting the leadership of Branson, whom we believe to be a classic Visionary Hero.

Branson seemed to be marked for special achievement at a young age. At graduation, his headmaster said, "Congratulations, Branson. I predict that you will either go to prison or become a millionaire."[8]

By nature, Branson is a shy man—but he has never hesitated to promote the Virgin brand through promotion of his products and his adventurous exploits. He has raced speedboats, flown hot air balloons, and jumped out of airplanes. He enjoys challenges, relishes being the underdog, and challenging the establishment.

Branson has often been praised for his skills in motivating his employees. His leadership, in fact, has been described as an extension of his personality. "Branson is good at surrounding himself with very talented people and creating the right environment for them to flourish."[9] He has a great deal of direct personal communication with his employees and a reputation for being very accessible. He is known as a corporate leader who loves his employees, treats them like family, inspires them to achieve great things, and empowers them to become great leaders.

Branson may have a touch of SuperLeadership but he's mainly a Visionary Hero. The strength of his leadership of Virgin is based on people wanting to follow Richard Branson the persona. His power is primarily inspirational. Employees' emotional commitment is based on Branson's vision. The important decisions at Virgin are mainly made by Branson. "Although I listen carefully to everyone, there are times when I make up my mind and just do it," he says of himself.[10]

Branson has achieved great success with his Visionary Hero leadership. He is a billionaire who has fame, celebrity status, wealth, friends, family, and fun. He is a gifted entrepreneur. Through his visionary leadership, he is a great motivator of people.

THE SUPERLEADER

The fourth view of leadership is the SuperLeader, one who leads others to lead themselves. The SuperLeader is also known as an *empowering* leader. With this type of leader, the focus is mainly on the followers. Leaders become "super"—possessing the strength and wisdom of many persons—by helping to unleash the abilities of the followers who surround them. The SuperLeader multiplies his/her own strength through the strength of others.

The leader's task becomes that of helping followers to develop their own self-leadership skills to contribute more fully to the organization. The SuperLeader encourages follower initiative, self-responsibility, self-confidence, self-goal-setting, positive opportunity thinking, and self-problem-solving. The SuperLeader encourages others to take responsibility rather than giving orders. One especially important part of the SuperLeadership challenge in the 21st century is to assure that followers have needed information and knowledge to exercise their own self-leadership.

The SuperLeadership perspective transcends heroic leadership. In the past, the idea of a leader implied that the spotlight was on the leader. With SuperLeadership the spotlight is placed on the follower. Followers, in turn, tend to experience exceptional commitment and ownership of their work.

 SuperLeadership is not permissiveness. It's an active form of leadership that encourages others to lead themselves.

Sometimes, people confuse empowerment with permissiveness. But the two are definitely not the same in the case of SuperLeadership. Follower self-leadership is not a permission or privilege, but a clearly focused strategy to empower through enhancing follower skill, confidence, and especially knowledge and information. Ensuring that knowledge and information is appropriately placed in an organization is critical to effective SuperLeadership. Bill Gates described the importance of "information . . . that enables knowledge workers to turn passive data into active information."[11] He emphasizes the role of information to empower rather than control. The leader of the 21st century is one who can create a company of self-leaders who have the knowledge and information to have a meaningful impact on their work and their organization.

IS ONE TYPE OF LEADERSHIP BEST?

We live in a competitive society and we often treat viewpoints and opinions in a competitive mode. For example, when discussing various types of leadership we often hear the question, "Which type is best?"

Well, we are clearly biased toward SuperLeadership, since this is what the book is about. But we recognize that the different types of leadership each have their own advantages. See the following chart for our views of the characteristics or outcomes generally found from each type of leadership.

Note that all of the four leadership types can be useful in influencing others. But only SuperLeadership has a long-term perspective that concentrates on the development of followers. Because leading others to lead themselves is such an important challenge for leadership in the 21st century, and the primary focus of this book, we will devote the remainder of this chapter to some overall Super-Leadership issues.

THE CHALLENGE OF SUPERLEADERSHIP

With SuperLeadership, the important twist in the leadership process is that followers are now treated as—and become—leaders. The apparent contradictions inherent in leading others to lead themselves require some mental adjustment. For example, if followers lead themselves, then is the leader really leading at all? Our answer is an emphatic yes, although the specific leader behaviors are quite

PREDICTABLE OUTCOMES OF FOUR LEADERSHIP TYPES

Strongman

- short-term compliance
- short-term learning
- low flexibility
- dissatisfaction
- high turnover
- long-term rebellion
- low innovation
- compliance

Transactor

- stable good performance
- satisfaction with pay
- low turnover
- low innovation
- low flexibility
- calculative, self-serving perspective
- compliance

Visionary Hero

- high performance
- enthusiasm
- long-term commitment
- emotional involvement
- difficulties in leader's absence caused by dependence or turnover if leader leaves
- problems if the leader's vision is incorrect or unethical

SuperLeader

- high long-term performance
- short-term confusion/ frustration
- high follower self-confidence
- high follower development
- very high flexibility
- high innovation
- ability to work in absence of leader
- teamwork

different. The leader is leading followers to be the best self-leaders they can be.

S *The apparent contradictions inherent in leading others to lead themselves require some mental adjustment. . . . This approach challenges leaders to rethink their fundamental assumptions about leadership and authority.*

In the long run, SuperLeadership can produce significant benefits in terms of increased performance, innovation, and fulfillment for leaders and followers (self-leaders) alike. Self-leadership is the engine and provides much of the energy required for success. Self-leadership is the essence of effective followership. SuperLeadership provides a context for self-leadership, a means of coordinating it among individuals, and a support mechanism for its development. In short, SuperLeaders inspire and facilitate self-leadership in their followers.

PUTTING SUPERLEADERSHIP INTO PRACTICE

How do we execute SuperLeadership? The ways for developing self-leadership in others can be divided up in many ways. One very broadbrush view for understanding the overall approaches for implementing SuperLeadership includes three general strategies: interpersonal strategies, team strategies, and organizational strategies.

Empowerment can be implemented through interpersonal strategies. That is, on a day-to-day basis the execution of SuperLeadership is mainly vested in the interpersonal verbal and nonverbal communications that occur between a leader and followers. The purpose of this leader-follower interaction emphasizes placing knowledge and information in the hands of the follower so that the follower can act with authority when needed.

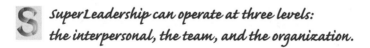

SuperLeadership can operate at three levels: the interpersonal, the team, and the organization.

Empowerment can also be implemented through team strategies. In fact, teams are the primary vehicle that contemporary organizations use to implement employee empowerment. Project, task force, concurrent engineering, cross-functional, top management, and self-directed teams are all team approaches to empowering others. Teams can be an extremely useful vehicle for launching self-leadership.

Finally, organizations can be changed to enhance the empowerment and self-leadership of others. For example, the notion of horizontal or flat organizations pushes responsibility down to the lowest levels. Network and virtual organizational designs are also consistent with the idea of SuperLeadership.

In summary, the essence of SuperLeadership is the challenge of leading followers to discover the potentialities that lie within themselves. In the following chapters, we concentrate on this theme: How can SuperLeaders lead others to lead themselves? The heart of SuperLeadership is follower self-leadership—the behavioral and cognitive strategies that each of us uses every day to influence our own behavior. Follower self-leadership is the main target of the SuperLeader's attention and action.

Chainsaw Al—
SuperLeader Not!

Abhishek Srivastava

In 30 years of corporate life, Albert J. Dunlap acquired nicknames such as "Chainsaw Al," "Rambo in Pinstripes," and "The Shredder," which aptly characterized his leadership as CEO of several companies. He would storm a company that was in distress, slash a significant proportion of its manpower, sell big chunks of its businesses, use this money to reduce debt, improve the stock price, set the company for sale, and move on to other companies—usually becoming richer in the process.

After graduating from West Point and serving three years in the military, Dunlap began his business career as a junior executive at Kimberly-Clark Corporation, a leading manufacturer of paper products. But he soon took advantage of an opportunity to run a company, even though he had not yet reached the age of 30. The owner of Sterling Pulp and Paper Company, Ely Meyer, was encountering considerable debt and severe problems of production. Meyer offered the young, ambitious Dunlap the opportunity to run Sterling, thus providing him the opportunity for his first lessons in turning around a poorly performing business.

THE "SLASH AND BURN" LEADER

His experience at Sterling began Dunlap's reign as a Strongman leader, marked by a string of slash-and-burn massacres at a variety of companies. He attacked the problems at Sterling in military fashion, reducing costs, laying off people, and pruning operations.

Later, in 1983, he was appointed CEO of Lily-Tulip Company, one of the largest suppliers of disposable cups to the food service industry. As he described in his autobiography, on the first day of his assignment at Lily-Tulip he called a brief meeting of the senior management. Based partly on information and partly on instinct, he pointed his index finger at the people he wanted to remain and said, "You two stay—the rest of you are fired. Goodbye."[1] In his three-year stay at Lily-Tulip he cut headquarters staff by 50 percent and salaried staff by 20 percent.[2]

His next assignment was with Crown-Zellerbach, a troubled timber company. This opportunity brought him in contact with Sir James Goldsmith, a European billionaire and statesman. Goldsmith was internationally known as a hostile-takeover artist. Dunlap mastered the slash-and-burn approach of quick turnaround under Goldsmith's mentoring. Dunlap acknowledged, "Sir James was a larger-than-life influence on me."[3] In his three years at Crown-Zellerbach, from 1986–89, Dunlap slashed distribution centers from 22 to four, and reduced staff by 22 percent.[4]

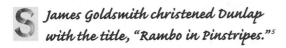

S James Goldsmith christened Dunlap with the title, "Rambo in Pinstripes."[5]

In his next assignment, at Australian National Industries, Dunlap reduced employment by 47 percent in 11 months, including a reduction of headquarters staff from 200 to 23. At Consolidated Press he sold off 300 of 413 companies.[6]

The crowning moment of Dunlap's slash-and-burn style came with his assignment to Scott Paper Company, the Philadelphia-based paper producer. On his third day, he fired nine of the firm's eleven top executives. Within a relatively short period of time, Dunlap eliminated more than 11,000 jobs, or a third of the payroll.[7] In 1995 Dunlap made a name for himself on Wall Street by selling Scott Paper to Kimberly-Clark Corporation for about $9 billion, or about three times the company's market value when he had taken over two years earlier. For less than two years' work he walked away with $100 million in salary, bonus, stock gains, and other perks.[8]

Dunlap had established a well-developed pattern, swiftly moving from one company to another, firing executives, slashing manpower, divesting businesses, improving the financials, and, eventually, selling the company. Interestingly, the popular media paid little attention to the rebuilding and reinvestment that seemed to be necessary after Chainsaw Al had departed.

SUNBEAM—CHAINSAW'S WATERLOO

The apparent success of Dunlap's leadership at Scott Paper earned him wide publicity. When it became public knowledge that he was taking charge of Sunbeam Corporation, the stock price soared. As a *Wall Street Journal* report points out, the stock rose not on expectation of growth but in anticipation of Dunlap's ability to downsize and quickly sell the company.[9] Dunlap took the reins of the company in July 1996, and five months later, in his typical style, announced elimination of nearly 50 percent of the company's 12,000 employees, sale or consolidation of 39 of its 53 facilities, and scrapping of 87 percent of Sunbeam's products.[10] The stock market euphoria continued until March 1998, when Sunbeam stock closed at a record high of $52 a share.

Until this point, at least on the surface, Dunlap's leadership seemed to be effective from a financial viewpoint. But the weaknesses of this very short-term perspective were about to rear their ugly heads. The first shoe fell on April 3, 1998, when Sunbeam stock fell by 25 percent after PaineWebber analyst Andrew Shore downgraded it.[11] This was in response to the company's shocking report of losses in the first quarter of 1998 after posting an impressive performance in 1997. On May 11, 1998, Dunlap told investors he had taken his eye "off the ball," and promised that it would "never happen again."[12] However, it was too late. On June 13, 1998, the directors of the board unceremoniously fired him from his position as chairman and CEO of Sunbeam. "We lost confidence in his leadership and his forecasts,"[13] said Peter A. Langerman, who led the revolt of the board of directors and was named chairman.

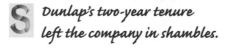

Dunlap's two-year tenure left the company in shambles.

Shortly after Dunlap's demise at Sunbeam, the company experienced an investigation by the Securities and Exchange Commission. Also, shareholder suits alleged that Sunbeam had pumped up its winter sales by selling products to retailers on attractive terms, with the understanding that they would be delivered later. Shareholders contended that they were misled about the company's health. Sunbeam sold $50 million worth of grills in December and allowed retailers until June to pay for them. Shareholders claimed that the promotion artificially inflated Sunbeam's fourth-quarter results of 1997 at the expense of the first quarter of 1998, as part of a plan to finance acquisitions.[14]

Although it was not known at that time, Dunlap was aggressively trying to push out more and more volume. As the company later acknowledged, he began to engage in so-called "bill and hold" deals with retailers, where Sunbeam products were purchased at large discounts and then held at third-party warehouses for delivery later. In fact, the company was left with so much excess inventory that it had to lease a World War II bomber plant in Tulsa, Oklahoma.[15] By booking these sales before the goods were delivered, Dunlap artificially boosted Sunbeam's revenues in 1997. In effect, he was shifting sales from 1998 to 1997. In a restatement of earnings issued four months after the departure of Dunlap, Sunbeam slashed the reported earnings of 1997 by 65 percent.[16] Thus, Dunlap's apparent success was simply the result of artificial and dubious accounting practices and, actually, the company had effectively been in the red in 1997.

Chainsaw's Trail of Tears

Dunlap held a very short-term view, both in terms of leadership of human resources and of the company's financial performance. Apparently he was simply eager to show immediate signs of turnaround to Wall Street. To accomplish this, Dunlap donned the cloak of a Strongman leader. He clearly did not inspire his subordinates with his vision nor did he share power. He may have influenced a few key followers through lucrative financial rewards contingent, of course, on their unquestioned loyalty. But more than anything else he wielded brute power from a position of absolute authority. In an online reader survey conducted by Business Week, a majority of nearly 500 readers evaluated Dunlap as an unimaginative, ruthless executive.[17]

Followers exposed to this kind of leadership invariably work under persistent fear of losing their jobs. As Dunlap proudly claimed, "employees never know what to expect from me, which keeps them on their toes."[18] A clear, intimidating message is sent to followers that they should either fall in line, or else fall out. As former Sunbeam vice president William Kirkpatrick put it, "When you work for Al it's not a career, it's a job."[19]

 At each of his stops, Dunlap had initiated a reign of terror and left a trail of tears.

Such leadership produces the fear-based compliance of "yes persons" plain and simple. All thinking under Dunlap was centralized—only he, a key consultant, and limited set of followers were the source of all ideas. Employees were mere numbers to be decimated at will. Consequently, employees do not think freely nor express their creative opinions. Dunlap assigned goals and thrust his decisions on the rest of the organization. He operated in a top-down fashion with strict control. There was no room for dissent. Like a typical military leader in the middle of a battle, he yelled out orders that his followers could not question. In his autobiography, Dunlap characterized his focus on rapid action in American Can as "Do it, dammit!"[20] He made it clear that if the job was not performed as commanded, employees could face punishment that was often as severe as dismissal.

Dunlap did pull off short-term turnarounds of several companies. But the long-term results of Al Dunlap's leadership are not admirable. Of the eight troubled outfits that he led, six are gone—sold off, split up, or otherwise no longer existing as independent entities. Two, in which his impact was not of the same scale as at Scott or Sunbeam, are still operated by an Australian investor. And while Scott was sold to Kimberly-Clark at a fat premium the deal went badly for the acquiring company, which was left to clean up the mess.[21]

As for Sunbeam, eight months after Dunlap's departure the *Wall Street Journal* named Sunbeam Corporation as the worst one-year performer of 1998.[22] The report mentioned that a $1000 investment in Sunbeam at the end of 1997 was worth only $163 at the end of 1998. Dunlap's kind of leadership may produce some desired results in the short run when the urgency of the situation is high and the degree of involvement desired from the subordinate is relatively low, but the long run is quite a different matter.

 A Strongman leader may bring some order for a short period. But the long run is quite a different matter.

In the end it appears that Dunlap's contributions consisted of little more than "smoke and mirrors" with temporary, artificial improvement and no real substance or investment in people for the future. Indeed, Dunlap is "Super-Leader—*NOT!*" Most of all, the adventures of Chainsaw Al reveal that the damage left in the wake of such a Strongman leader can take years to repair.

3 SuperLeadership 101:
The Basics for Unleashing Self-Leadership

"**I JUST DON'T UNDERSTAND** this new generation! I don't think I expect too much from my people. I just want them to be good followers. It seems like no one is interested in being a good follower anymore," Brent concluded with a tone of despair.

"I agree that followership is important, Bill, but maybe you are too concerned about members of your department following rather than leading," Mary responded calmly.

"Don't get me wrong Mary. I do believe in empowerment but I *am* the manager here, and I believe that I need to be the one that provides the leadership, the vision and direction for our efforts. I feel I do a pretty good job of that but I still find that my employees try to head off in directions I never asked them to. It makes things seem kind of chaotic and I don't like it. And frankly I don't understand what you mean about the need to be concerned about leading as opposed to following. I'm the leader here! Is there anybody that doesn't understand that?"

"Brent—the way I look at it, the world has become too complex and changable for there to be only one leader in any organizational unit anymore. Everyone needs to be fully contributing from their unique experiences and expertise, and to me that means that everyone needs to be doing some leading, especially of themselves."

"Leading themselves? Now you really have me confused, Mary. Leaders lead and followers follow. I do believe that good followers not only do what a leader directs them to do but also try to anticipate what the leader wants. Just what do you mean by leading themselves?"

"To me, the key to effective leadership in any organization is good self-leadership. I believe that we are all our own most important leaders and that we need to make good choices regarding how we can best contribute, given our talents and abilities. I also believe that those individuals that are designated as leaders have a crucial responsibility to lead others to lead themselves. The best leadership comes from within, and is directed at the person we see in the mirror every day."

"I must admit you have me interested, Mary. I know I need to do something different and it is getting harder and harder to cope with all the technological changes that have been implemented recently. Much of my communication is now through e-mail and most of my people spend much of their time working away from the office. I'll tell you what. I'll buy you lunch if you'll share more about this idea of self-leadership with me."

"Well it is about time for lunch and you do seem to need some of my wisdom," Mary responded playfully. "OK, it's a deal."

How can SuperLeaders guide followers to discover their own potential? How can SuperLeaders help their followers to become positive and effective self-leaders? One of the first steps is to understand self-leadership: the way each of us influences ourselves to enhance our own satisfaction and performance. When we understand self-leadership, we can then concentrate on how we can help others to become better self-leaders. Think about this challenge for yourself: What can I do to lead others to lead themselves?

In this chapter, we introduce the fundamentals of SuperLeadership. We begin with some basic ideas about self-leadership. Then, we present an approach to leading others that provides a foundation for others to lead themselves. We also address some basic issues in regard to implementing these ideas, and identify the situations when this leadership approach is most appropriate. In subsequent chapters, we follow up by describing in more detail the specifics of

SuperLeadership and how it applies to individual followers, to teams, and to organizational cultures.

SELF-LEADERSHIP AS A PERSONAL CHARACTERISTIC

How much of an employee's self-leadership skill can originate from within? Are self-leaders born or are they made? Can self-leadership skills be taught by a leader or an organization?

Certainly genetic predisposition, family background, schooling and professional training, and the general social environment all have some impact on the self-leadership that individuals initially bring to an organization. Most leaders would prefer to hire people who come from a background that teaches strong self-discipline. Consider Robert and Ben:

Robert and Ben came to work for Harry during the same week, after they had both graduated from the Department of Systems Engineering at the state university. Within three months, Harry was able to observe substantial differences in the way Robert and Ben handled their jobs. Robert had devised his own project control system. He developed an Internet-based personal management and reminder system that kept track of his own target dates for his projects, along with his coded notations of the work that had been completed on each project. In addition, Robert's information system featured a weekly reminder list that popped up on his computer screen every time he signed on. Whenever Harry asked Robert about a specific project, Robert usually had the answer within a minute or so after calling up his system. And Robert really thrived on his work. He really seemed to be motivated to perform well and enjoyed expending the effort to do so.

Ben was just the opposite. While Ben was as capable an engineer as Robert, Harry had difficulties keeping track of Ben's progress on his projects—mainly because Ben himself was so sloppy about target dates and keeping track of the work he had accomplished. Ben had difficulty adapting his work to the interconnected database of the division, and always seemed to be troubled by a "lost" file.

In discussing Robert and Ben with his boss, Harry remarked: "Robert is excellent at controlling his own activities. He sets his own goals, he is aware of his progress and he displays obvious commitment to his work. He learns from his mistakes. Most of all, he's developed his own way of interfacing with the division database so that he knows how to quickly acquire the information he needs, and how to organize that information in a usable way. Ben, on the other hand, is having problems. He has very little awareness of the current status of his projects, still has trouble linking with the database, and I have to keep on top of him. I question his commitment to reaching his full performance potential. One of my main projects over the next six months is to teach self-leadership skills to Ben. His fundamental technical skills are just too good for us to lose."

Robert E. Kelley was one of the first to recognize that the new knowledge worker is a different breed, and requires a different type of leadership. More than a decade ago he emphasized the need for organizations to adapt to the special needs and demands of the new knowledge worker. He emphasized that the new worker deals in knowledge, not just physical labor or goods and services. He said of the new generation:

They are imaginative and original. . . . They engage in complex problem solving, not bureaucratic drudgery or mechanical routine . . . and have little tolerance for boredom. [They demand] interesting work and satisfying emotional relationships . . . [and] psychic and social stimulation on the [job]. . . . Taking orders . . . insults their intelligence and often results in a creative shutdown. . . . [They prefer to] manage themselves.[1]

More recently, a cover of *Forbes* magazine featured a picture of the management guru Peter Drucker with the words in large print, "Everything you learned is wrong." Inside the magazine Drucker addresses the impact of the rise of knowledge workers in eliminating the concept of "subordinates." He explains that the rising use of the term "associate" is not just polite or cosmetic; rather, it is a recognition of reality. Drucker points out that "knowledge workers must know more about their job than their boss does—or what good are they?"[2] All this of course has vast implications for leadership— knowledge workers must be better equipped and allowed to lead themselves.

 Our basic theme is that self-leadership can be taught, encouraged, and maintained by a SuperLeader.

Indeed, organizations of the 21st century should develop new selection practices that feature strong consideration of a potential employee's self-leadership. But to be realistic, not every employee comes with a fully developed repertoire of self-leadership skills. Indeed, our basic theme is that self-leadership can be taught, encouraged, and maintained by a SuperLeader. Furthermore, we believe that this objective can be approached in a systematic, proven way: *there are specific actions that organizations and leaders can take to develop the self-leadership capabilities of employees.* The fundamental key, of course, is to begin by adopting the philosophy of SuperLeadership, that every follower has the potential to enhance his or her own self-leadership if provided with the proper leadership in this direction. Desiring self-led employees is not sufficient. Widespread self-leadership needs to filter down from the top, to be ingrained in the culture of the organization. Learning to be a Super-Leader is the key ingredient in teaching self-leadership to employees.

SHIFTING TO SELF-LEADERSHIP

Especially in the beginning of an employee's career with an organization, the SuperLeader must provide orientation, guidance, and direction. The need for specific direction at the beginning stages of employment stems from two sources. First, new employees are unfamiliar with the objectives, tasks, and procedures of their positions. They have not yet fully developed their task abilities. But more pertinent to our discussion, new employees are not likely to have an adequate set of self-leadership skills.

Note that we do not conclude that all leaders should completely relinquish influence over followers, nor do we presume that every human is endowed with a fully developed set of self-leadership skills. On the contrary, we generally believe that only a minority of individuals in our society has had the natural opportunity to fully develop their own self-leadership. Indeed, many institutions (family, schools, military service) inadvertently promote and encourage dependence rather than self-sufficiency. Individuals learn to become accustomed to authority figures making decisions and influencing their behavior in even the smallest details. Thus, the role of Super-Leaders becomes critical; they play the pivotal role of shifting others from dependence to independence.

 *Self-leadership can be learned.*

How is this done? We recommend a procedure that consists of (1) initial modeling, (2) guided participation, and (3) gradual development of self-leadership.[3] We will begin with a brief discussion of each of the phases of teaching others to lead themselves.

Initial Modeling

The importance of modeling cannot be underestimated. It is a demonstration of self-leadership to others. Those who are currently effective self-leaders serve as a model from which others learn self-leadership. Even if unintentional, the SuperLeader's self-leadership behavior inevitably serves as a model to followers. For example, an executive who is overly dependent on superiors would serve as a poor self-leadership model. We would likely find a similar pattern of overdependence in that executive's followers.

"Management of self is critical; without it, leaders and managers can do more harm than good."

—**Warren Bennis**[4]

Thus the first step in teaching self-leadership to others is to *practice* self-leadership—to *be* a self-leader. This means practicing self-leadership, physically and mentally, and doing so in a vivid and recognizable manner that can serve as a model for others. Employees will adopt the standards that they observe in exemplary models and then evaluate their own performance according to those standards. Thus, as one example, leaders who "stretch" themselves with challenging goals are likely to evoke the same sort of achievement-oriented behavior in followers. Conversely, executives who are satisfied with mediocre accomplishments for themselves are likely to see the same mediocre achievements by followers.

Even if unintentional, the SuperLeader's self-leadership behavior inevitably serves as a model to followers.

Guided Participation

Guided participation is when the follower first attempts self-leadership, but in a more safe and controlled environment. The leader is still there to guide and advise the follower. In this phase, the verbal behavior of SuperLeaders is critical. For example, they can attempt to evoke self-leadership among their followers through a series of directed questions. While specific self-leadership strategies are discussed more fully in Chapters 4, 5, and 6, here we provide examples of questions that foster some of those strategies.

To facilitate self-observation, questions such as "Do you know how well you are doing?" or "How about keeping a record of how many times that happens?" are appropriate.

To facilitate self-set goals, the SuperLeader might ask: "How many will you shoot for?" "When do you want to have it finished?" "What will your target be?"

To promote self-evaluation leading to self-reward: "How do you think you did?" "Are you pleased with the way it went?" "Why don't you try it out?" and "Let's practice that" are appropriate remarks to stimulate rehearsals.

To spur thought-focused self-leadership, questions to ask might include: "How do you like your job?" "Have you thought about trying different ways of doing it that you might enjoy more?" "What opportunities do you see in the current problems you face?"

The verbal communication of SuperLeaders is critical.

Questions such as these combined with constructive suggestions, instruction, and coaching on effective self-leadership, can provide the necessary guidance to ignite the self-leadership flame in others. The aim, of course, is to give employees practice in thinking about and then implementing their own self-leadership behaviors.

The special implications of this process are that the guidance, evaluation, and reward functions are gradually shifted from external sources to the individual; the progress made in self-leadership is reinforced and a shift is made from external rewards to self-administered rewards.

Gradual Development of Self-Leadership

An important part of SuperLeadership is shifting personal reward patterns as the follower becomes more and more capable of self-leadership. Initially, the SuperLeader rewards specific *performance-*related behaviors by the follower. As time goes by, the rewards shift from performance associated with the task to the process of self-leadership itself. In other words, the SuperLeader emphasizes self-leadership rather than specific task-related behavior.

The primary function of the SuperLeader becomes one of encouraging, guiding, and rewarding an employee's self-leadership practice rather than *directly* providing instructions and rewards for performance. Some executives may resist this shift because, on first impression, it creates the illusion of having *less* control over followers. Over the long run, however, this shift from direct (short-term) control to follower self-leadership is highly desirable. In the long term, the overall effectiveness of followers will be improved as a result of their increased self-leadership ability. In turn, the leader will enjoy the benefits of SuperLeadership, such as more time, more committed employees, an increase in innovative ideas from followers, and a newfound power for progress that flows from working with more fully developed self-leaders.

 Over time, the SuperLeader emphasizes self-leadership rather than concentrating on specific task-related behavior.

In this phase, it is particularly important that social rewards be given when employee self-leadership behavior does occur. This means that establishing a culture in which each employee supports and believes in self-leadership behavior is crucial. Unfortunately, other sources might detract from the development of effective self-leadership; peers, for example, can encourage overconformity. Thus, verbal encouragement and other forms of support from the Super-Leader are critical in establishing the initiative that comes from self-leadership.

WHEN SHOULD LEADERS ENCOURAGE FOLLOWER SELF-LEADERSHIP

Overall, we strongly believe that moving employees toward self-leadership is advantageous to an organization. Nevertheless, it is naive to assume that relying on self-leadership is *always* appropriate. External executive control will likely always have a role in any organization. Also, it is incorrect to assume that self-leadership and external control are mutually exclusive. Even in the most intensive external-control situations, employees always exercise some degree of self-leadership. Conversely, even when self-leadership is deliberately encouraged, some external control, primarily focused on productive task results, is commonly found and typically wanted by employees. In addition, rewarding the self-leadership process itself is usually necessary to make it work.

Several important situational factors influence the appropriateness of attempts to develop self-leadership in followers: (1) the nature of the task, (2) the availability of time, and (3) the importance of developing people.

The Nature of the Task

The nature of the task itself is connected with the potential value of self-leadership. For example, technology can place a limitation on how much follower discretion is possible. Traditional assembly lines, for example, allow less discretion than several other approaches to performing work. A managerial decision to "enrich" a job usually is concerned directly with the issue of self-leadership in one form or another. Also, it seems clear that when the task is largely creative, analytical, or intellectual in nature, greater self-leadership is appropriate.

 Most of all, when the task is clearly connected with "knowledge" the exercise of self-leadership is at a premium.

The basic "transaction" of a knowledge worker's job consists of adding value to information through creativity, ideas, and experience. The "coin of the realm" for knowledge workers is information, and knowledge workers need the discretion that stems from self-leadership if they are to perform at their capacity.

Self-leadership might be viewed as falling on an employee-empowerment continuum. Managers must make decisions as to how much self-leadership to encourage in followers, and some types of problems are more appropriate for self-leadership than others. In general, more empowering decision methods are appropriate when:

- The problem is unstructured.

- Information is needed from followers.

- Solutions must be accepted by followers to ensure implementation.

- Followers share organizational goals.[5]

Another task situation that calls for self-leadership is one where employees work remotely, with minimal contact with the manager. Examples include "telecommuters" working out of their homes and salespersons in the field. Through the Internet, many employees are part of a networked organization where they undertake "distributive" work—that is, tasks that are technically linked yet done at different locations or different times. Many employees today are members of virtual teams, where direct day-to-day leadership is not possible. In all of these situations employees need to be empowered and capable self-leaders if they are to perform to their potential.

The Availability of Time

The time available for decision making or problem solving is another element that has a bearing on whether self-leadership should be encouraged. In crisis situations the time simply may not be available to develop self-leadership capabilities. When the building is on fire, it's no time for a participative decision-making session. Highly directive or perhaps transformational leadership might be most appropriate. There is a time and a place for the Strongman type of leadership, especially if the ground work for effective self-leadership has not been fully completed when a crisis occurs.

S *If an employee is likely to encounter a future crisis in the absence of a leader, then self-leadership training* now *would be appropriate.*

If an organization prepares in the proper way, then the best way to meet a crisis is with highly self-motivated self-leaders. The power of the fully capable self-leader to meet a crisis is incredible.

The Importance of Followers' Development

At opposite extremes are the "development" mode and the "short-term efficiency" mode. In the efficiency mode, self-leadership will be de-emphasized in order to speedily carry out the task in the most efficient manner possible. In this situation, directive or boss type leadership can be appropriate. Or, in urgent situations, Visionary Hero leadership might be most useful. Conversely, in the development mode, followers' self-leadership will be emphasized, encouraged, and regarded as an investment for the future. This stance might be termed *leader investment behavior*, from which a later return is expected. Note that we do *not* equate efficiency with long-term effectiveness.

Most executives operate in some zone between these two extremes. In the end, each executive must evaluate the specific situation. Factors such as the individual employee's eagerness and present capacity for self-leadership are important.

A NOTE OF CAUTION ABOUT
TOO MUCH CAUTION

While we strongly believe that different situations call for different actions on the part of leaders, we would like to make our overall conclusions clear. There is a danger in being overly cautious in diagnosing the need for self-leadership.

It's all too easy to underestimate the capabilities of seemingly ordinary people. There is a classic story about how Lincoln Electric, the highly successful welding manufacturing firm, found some special capabilities among its employees when it found its sales sagging. Faced with a no-layoff policy, it asked its factory workers for some help. Fifty of its production factory workers volunteered to help out in sales.

After a quickie training course in sales, the former production workers started calling on body shops all over the country. They concentrated on small shops that would be able to use the company's small welder. The end of the story is that their efforts brought in several million in new sales and established the small welder as one of Lincoln's core products.[6]

Lincoln Electric was relying on the idea of the self-fulfilling prophecy. *Real* SuperLeaders are willing to bet on their followers if there is even a little evidence that they can handle situations without imposing external constraints. Since they are willing to *take a risk* on people, success frequently becomes self-fulfilling. Such choices will not always pay off. But in the long run, most followers will become stronger if they are given plenty of opportunities to try out their own ideas, and sometimes fail, in their work. Invariably they will come up with different ways of doing things, including some that the leader may not feel totally comfortable with. In the end, however, the team will benefit from more committed, innovative employees who have been given the chance to shape their jobs to their own unique perspectives and capabilities and to grow in the process.

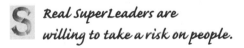

Real SuperLeaders are willing to take a risk on people.

Perhaps the most crucial question to ask in the short run is, "Can my follower benefit from a reliance on self-leadership in this situation without causing significant performance problems for the organization?" If the answer is yes, the burden of proof ought to be on why she *shouldn't* be allowed the freedom and given the guidance to be a self-leader. The *default* decision should be to move toward self-leadership. By acting this way, leaders are instilling a sense of confidence in their followers and introducing forces that can ultimately lead to self-fulfilling employee effectiveness. After all, they are being treated as though the leader feels they are dependable, competent people. If this approach is adopted, in the long run leaders will frequently be amazed by the positive results and asking, "What will our people think of next in moving us to new levels of performance?"

There will always be so-called rational reasons for not allowing employees to practice significant self-leadership. A SuperLeader will nevertheless be willing to take the risks necessary to provide the opportunity for followers to grow—and they will respond in remarkable ways. Our advice is straight and simple: when there is a *reasonable* potential for SuperLeadership, the bias should be in the direction of enhancing follower self-leadership. The most important point is, when SuperLeadership is given some time to work, in the long run the results will be substantial.

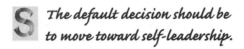

> The default decision should be
> to move toward self-leadership.

Usually, leaders think in terms of job-oriented behaviors or specific tasks that an employee should perform. But a true Super-Leader thinks beyond immediate performance-oriented behaviors. The major objective of the SuperLeader is to improve the *self-leadership* capability of followers. Later, we explore SuperLeadership strategies in some detail. Again, the point to emphasize is that a SuperLeader is mainly focused on leading others to lead themselves.

SHIFTING FROM DEPENDENCE TO INDEPENDENCE

A SuperLeader follows a straightforward, underlying theme in attempting to develop the self-leadership skills of employees: shifting employees from dependence on external management to independence. The lists on the next page give examples of specific ways that traditional management functions can be shifted according to this theme.

The following chapters provide specifics on how this shift from dependence to independence can be undertaken.

> A SuperLeader follows a straightforward, underlying theme...
> shifting employees from dependence...to independence.

FROM	To
▶ external observation	▶ self-observation
▶ assigned goals	▶ self-set goals
▶ external reinforcement for task performance	▶ internal reinforcement plus external reinforcement for self-leadership behaviors
▶ motivation mainly based on external compensation	▶ motivation also based on the "natural"rewards of the work
▶ external criticism	▶ self-criticism
▶ external problem solving	▶ self-problem solving
▶ external planning	▶ self-planning
▶ external task design	▶ self-design of tasks
▶ obstacle thinking	▶ opportunity thinking
▶ compliance to the organization's vision	▶ commitment to a vision that the follower helped to create

Remember, a fundamental reason for shifting from dependence to independence is to improve bottom-line indicators such as productivity and quality while the follower benefits as well. Clearly, this would not be possible unless every employee was considered a true self-leader.

SuperLeading Individuals, Teams, and Organizations

The overall SuperLeadership framework consists of several basic components. First, self-leadership serves as the core and focus of the process. A SuperLeader concentrates on developing the self-leadership of followers as a means of achieving overall organizational effectiveness. SuperLeaders work at developing self-leadership at all levels of the organization: self-leadership of the individual, self-leading teams, and a total organizational culture of self-leadership.

SuperLeadership is not the province of a select few who were fortunate enough to be endowed with special skills. Anyone can be a SuperLeader to at least some degree. In the following chapters, we lay out the path toward more effective leadership and performance for both leaders and followers. We provide a means to discover how to lead others to lead themselves.

We begin this process by learning more about leading ourselves. The next three chapters focus on self-leadership, the influence we exercise over ourselves in order to perform better. We concentrate on self-leadership through: (1) behavior and action, (2) natural rewards, and (3) the mind.

PROFILE

Percy Barnevik
of ABB

In 1987, few would have predicted the remarkable success that followed the merger of two sleepy European engineering firms.[1] Percy Barnevik, until recently CEO of ABB (Asea Brown Boveri, originally of Sweden), was the architect of the merger that formed the giant worldwide engineering and power organization.

Barnevik's leadership has been widely recognized as something special. From our viewpoint, we see him as a combination of Visionary Hero and SuperLeader—Visionary Hero because of the astonishing growth that has resulted in more than 100 acquisitions and the addition of 100,000 employees to the payroll, and SuperLeader because of his championing of a new form of decentralization that places significant responsibility in the hands of local managers. The concept is called *multidomesticity*: "Think global, act local."

Barnevik has espoused an extremely flattened form of organization, with no more than five people between the CEO and the lowest level. According to Barnevik, "The fundamental organizational design . . . is known for its extreme decentralization. This . . . has been a theme throughout my whole career. . . . What I have tried to do is recreate small-company dynamism and creativity by building 5000 profit centers and 1300 legal entities. I have made an effort to reduce the layers." According to Manfred F. R. Kets de Vries, "Barnevik [has] created organizational structures where people have a sense of control and a feeling of ownership over what they do."

The principles of SuperLeadership seem to be embedded in Barnevik's philosophy of leadership. For example, he believes in extending the capabilities of followers: "I want my people to constantly test their imagination [and] creative spirit. . . . We really have no choice but to create an . . . atmosphere where people can speak their minds."

S *"I believe there is tremendous potential in . . . people that is not exploited. . . . There is a whole new avenue for developing human potential."*

—Percy Barnevik

Underlying all of this is an undying optimistic belief in people.

Moreover, he sees the development of others as providing his greatest personal motivation: " . . . What gives me the greatest satisfaction is seeing [the] people whom I have promoted succeed. Then you have created something that will . . . last."

Barnevik also believes in teams: "We are . . . cutting out a whole layer of . . . supervision to give teams more responsibility. . . . I think there is huge potential here. . . ."

As one example, in 1990 ABB launched a continuous improvement program called "T50." This effort was designed to create flexible work operations that will continue to develop and improve, even when performance is currently strong. This continuous improvement strategy combines cycle time reduction (the original objective was 50 percent, hence the label "T50"), employee competence development, and decentralization, all centered on an overriding customer focus.

An example of the results of this process was a new work design in the unit that assembles electrical push buttons. This unit had experienced a variety of problems, including unreliable delivery times, high turnover and absenteeism, and employee boredom and burnout. Once the pilot T50 program had been put in place, results improved dramatically. The essence of the program entailed high employee involvement in a team setting. Order cycle time went from twelve days to one, rejects from 15 percent to 1 percent, on-time delivery from 10 percent to 98 percent, turnover from 39 percent to 0 percent, absenteeism from 14 percent to 8 percent, and overall productivity increased 15 percent. Moreover, the control unit has experienced continued improvement. Thus, with a concrete success model to draw upon ABB has continued to roll out the T50 program throughout its international operations.

In a visit to Sweden, Charles Manz had an opportunity to visit one of ABB's Swedish operations (ABB Flakt Industri) and to interview division president Anders Wahrolen. Mr. Wahrolen has been extensively involved with the T50 program. During the interview, Wahrolen's comments focused primarily on total systems issues. He considered employee empowerment as a fundamental key to the process—he seemed to consider it to be simple common sense to involve teams of employees if high performance is desired. He described how the supervisor-to-worker ratio had changed, from 1–7 to 1–50. He further explained that as part of the company's commitment to individual employee competency, every employee is required to construct a personal development plan. In addition, employee training is matched to the developmental areas identified by each individual in his or her plan. Wahrolen also indicated that there was some tough negotiating over goals or benchmarks in the company, and emphasized that all levels need to have significant input into their own goals.

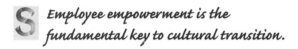

S *Employee empowerment is the fundamental key to cultural transition.*

Wahrolen acknowledges the importance of recognizing cultural differences in any work design application. He noted in particular his perception of significant differences between how Americans seemed to view the results of new organizational designs versus how Swedes viewed them. He explained that at international conferences he frequently found that American accounts of the success of new organizational designs seemed to be "overly optimistic." He believes Swedes take a "more humble" stance, tending to describe their results as not being as good as they really are. It was apparent from his low-key demeanor that he was no exception to this observation. He described the very impressive results of the T50 program in a factual, unemotional tone. While he personally was conservative about what ABB has accomplished through empowered and ever-increasingly competent people, the impressive results of this model speak loud and clear. ABB has clearly made a significant transition toward creating a company where self-leadership is the norm.

Both Barnevik and Wahrolen clearly believe in leading others to lead themselves. From his view atop the giant ABB, Barnevik saw flat organizational structures and teams as critical foundations to empower others. Through his actions, Barnevik clearly lived the philosophy and behavior of the SuperLeader.

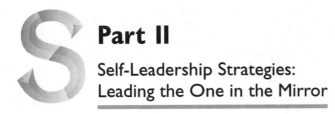

Part II

Self-Leadership Strategies: Leading the One in the Mirror

He who gains victory over other men is strong;
but he who gains a victory over himself is all powerful.
Lao-Tzu[1]

4 Self-Leadership in Action

YOU ARE DEEPLY SETTLED into the conference room chair as you listen to Bart, the new division general manager (and your boss). This is the first meeting between Bart and his staff, and he is outlining some of his philosophy and ideas about how he expects the division to be managed. You are new yourself, having assumed the position of department manager only two weeks ago.

Both you and Bart have been brought into the division as part of an attempt to salvage an organization that has been in the red for the last three years. You haven't worked for Bart before, but you hear through the grapevine that he has a record as a top-notch performer.

"One of the most important attributes by which I judge managers," says Bart, "is how good they are at self-leadership. Are they able to lead themselves?"

As you sit, you wonder what he really means by "self-leadership."

How about you? Do you believe the most important leadership you exercise is over the person staring back at you when you look in the mirror? Are you an effective self-leader? What *is* self-leadership?

S *The idea of self-leadership provides a new definition of followership.*

The core of SuperLeadership—leading others to lead themselves—is self-leadership. Self-leadership is the influence we exert over ourselves in order to perform better. A SuperLeader inspires and facilitates self-leadership in others. And a core of our philosophy is that in order to lead others, you must first learn to lead yourself. In this chapter and the next two, we address the topic of self-leadership in detail, to lay the foundation for addressing Super-Leadership throughout the remainder of the book.[1]

Based on our years of studying and advising employees and executives in many work settings, at many organizational levels, three basic assumptions underlie our ideas on self-leadership. First, everyone practices self-leadership to some degree, but not everyone is an effective self-leader. Second, *effective* self-leadership can be learned and thus is not restricted to people we intuitively describe as being "born" self-starters, self-directed, or self-motivated. And third, self-leadership is relevant to executives, managers, and nonmanagers alike—that is, to anyone who works.

There are different categories of self-leadership strategies. The first, discussed in this chapter, focuses on effective action. In the next two chapters we focus on strategies that use natural rewards, and promote effective thinking and feeling.

SuperLeadership inspires and facilitates self-leadership in others.

SELF-LEADERSHIP STRATEGIES FOR EFFECTIVE ACTION

The majority stockholder and manager of a small commuter airline found himself in a profit squeeze. Many of his competitors had already gone out of business. In addition to the countless duties involved in managing the firm on a daily basis, including personally flying some of the routes, he was convinced he needed a new, larger plane to operate more profitably. Somehow he managed to juggle the details of his job while putting together a creative financing plan for acquiring the plane he needed. This plan, along with adoption of several other changes, including rerouting his flight patterns, kept his firm on a growth trend in the face of pressures toward decline.

How does he do it? How does he put out the daily fires and still manage to introduce new, innovative ways of doing business? Much of the answer lies in his action-oriented self-leadership practices.

First, he uses the strategy of self-observation by keeping a detailed log or record of how he spends his time. In his pocket he carries a small portable computer "organizer" to do this. A few times a day, he uses a wireless connection to interface with his main business computer to exchange data and bring his records up to date. He also keeps a record of what he says to others over the phone regarding business matters, to help him be consistent in his future dealings with these people. In addition, he has adopted various cueing strategies to help him manage his performance. Once a week, being still a bit old-fashioned, he prints out in large type the notes that will serve as a reminder and a guide for his work efforts. He posts this printout right above his desk. He keeps a separate "follow up" file. He frequently rehearses what he will say during important phone calls before dialing. And he makes use of self-rewards. He enjoys reviewing his accomplishments against his goals and mentally rewarding himself for his achievements. As he puts it, "Self-gratification—that's what it's all about."[2]

We have seen variations of these same strategies in use in many different work settings. Following are some details about using additional self-leadership strategies including self-set goals, management of cues, rehearsal, self-observation, self-rewards, and self-correcting feedback.

Self-Set Goals

Goals are an important part of successful self-leadership. Setting goals, for both immediate work tasks and longer-term career achievements, establishes the basis for self-direction and establishing priorities. Limiting informal e-mail communications to forty-five minutes of a normal workday might be a reasonable self-set goal for someone who has a problem with excessive electronic chatting. Similarly, making six sales calls a day or increasing sales by eight percent for the fiscal quarter might be a self-set goal for someone in sales. Earning an MBA degree (by taking evening on-line classes) or becoming a vice president are examples of longer-term career goals. Much of the research on goal setting suggests that goals should be challenging but achievable and specific in order to have an optimal effect.

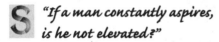 *"If a man constantly aspires, is he not elevated?"*
—Henry David Thoreau[3]

Management of Cues

Managing cues in our immediate work environment can help trigger constructive activities and reduce or eliminate destructive ones. Resigning from those annoying and distracting unnecessary electronic mailing lists, having phone calls held during specific times of the workday, eliminating distracting noises by closing the door, or even surrounding ourselves with talented people who bring out our best, all reflect different cueing strategies. An office, for example, can be decorated and equipped with things that stimulate performance. Simple devices such as installing an inspiring screensaver on our computer, or placing motivating plaques or pictures on the walls, can be helpful to some people. Posting the message "Are you using your time effectively right now?" in full view is a cue for effective time management. In fact, the time-management movement over the last few decades is largely based on cueing strategies.

David Packard, cofounder of Hewlett-Packard, described how, as a young man, he used a daily schedule as a cueing strategy to organize his own efforts. "I was resolved that I was going to have everything organized, so as a freshman I had a schedule set for every day ... what I was going to do every hour of the day . ..and times set up in the morning to study certain things....You did have to allocate your time, because as you know, there are a lot of things to do."[4] Packard was a man before his time, a customer-in-waiting for the invention of the Palm Pilot!

As we go deeper into the electronic age, technology seems to be making us more isolated. More and more people work out of their homes or at remote work sites and much communication takes place electronically. This can rob us of the important cues we receive from one another through face-to-face interaction. Of course one solution is video conferencing, or to equip our computers with software and devices such as digital cameras that enable us to electronically relate on a more personal level. Nevertheless, there is no substitute for physical, face-to-face interaction. To facilitate this valuable component of working with others requires more personal strategies, such as scheduling an informal monthly breakfast with other employees.

This is an age-old strategy that was used by former 3M CEO William McKnight during the early foundational years that led to that company's rise to prominence. On Saturday mornings he would join 3M employees in the employee cafeteria for an elbow-to-elbow breakfast that allowed him the kind of direct personal contact that provided encouragement for him and his workforce. Similarly, Bill Hewlett, co-founder of Hewlett-Packard, was noted for his extensive interaction with others at HP as part of his daily management style. Both of these examples reveal cueing strategies that provide opportunities to enhance an executive's informal information network.

Rehearsal

Rehearsal or practice is another useful self-leadership strategy. Practice is natural for improvement in golf or tennis—it should be just as natural in other parts of life, including work. Thinking through and practicing important tasks before they are done "for keeps" can contribute significantly to performance. Rehearsing a crucial formal presentation about a new Internet business to be made to a venture capitalist is an obvious example of this strategy. But many less formal activities are potential occasions for practice. A few minutes of mental rehearsal before calling on clients, practicing sensitive parts of an employee's performance review, going over the key steps required to safely and efficiently start up a machine, are all appropriate ways of using a rehearsal strategy. Role playing, for example, is commonly used in performance-appraisal training.

Self-Observation

Self-observation provides the necessary information—the life-blood—for effective self-leadership. By observing our behavior we can discover some clues about what needs to change and how to go about it. A simple record of what leads to a targeted behavior, its frequency, how long it lasts, and when it does or does not occur, can provide a wealth of information.

For example, if an employee is dissatisfied with her level of productivity she can observe, and briefly record on a personal organizer, notes about nonproductive behaviors. These behaviors might include informal conversations, unnecessary busywork, time spent surfing the Web, and so on. Also she could keep a record of the frequency and duration of these behaviors and the events that distracted more productive efforts. If these observations eventually disclose that an average of 17 hours a week are spent on informal conversations, an obvious problem has been identified. Also, if the records indicate that most of this chatting is triggered by trips to the department coffee machine, steps can be taken to limit this behavior, such as keeping a small coffee maker in her office. (However, she should be careful: coffee-machine conversations can provide rich interpersonal exchanges of information and knowledge.)

Self-observation also provides information for self-evaluations.

By analyzing the information that she has collected, she sets the stage for personally assessing the effectiveness of her work efforts.

Self-Rewards

Whatever we receive for our efforts has a major impact on our motivation and choices of future activities. Typically, the rewards received from the organization and others become the focus of attention, but self-rewards (and criticisms) can be just as important.

 Using self-rewards can be an especially powerful strategy for creating motivation to do tasks we find difficult or unappealing.

These self-rewards can be concrete and physical, like a nice dinner out or a lazy afternoon sailing on the bay after completing an especially challenging task. Taking a weekend at the beach as a reward for finally working the bugs out of the new office computer system, or after making a big sale, can help motivate future successes. Sometimes we can deliberately put aside a self-reward until a particular task has been accomplished. The rewards can also be private, mental creations such as imagining a favorite vacation spot or the future success and benefits resulting from successful work efforts. Intentionally providing ourselves with both physical and mental rewards for high performance can help sustain motivation and effort.

Self-Correcting Feedback (Not Self-Punishment)

Self-correcting feedback can also be part of the process, although the related practice of self-punishment generally is not very effective. Actually, most self-punishment is mental or cognitive in nature. A mild degree of guilt can sometimes be useful, but when it becomes excessive or habitual it can undermine motivation and effort. Habitual guilt and self-criticism can seriously damage self-confidence and self-esteem, and even lead to depression. The key is to study patterns of self-criticism by asking, for example, "Do I focus on destructive self-punishment or constructive corrective feedback? Does my self-criticism help or hinder my performance?" An introspective self-examination of a failure, trying to learn from it, providing constructive self-corrective feedback and refocusing energy on feeling good about accomplishments, represents a better alternative.

S *Self-rewards and corrective feedback are important ingredients of self-leadership, and are as important as rewards and criticisms received from others.*

Of course, ignoring our negative choices when we are obviously behaving and performing in undesirable ways can be a problem as well. There are times when a good self-scolding is appropriate. Generally, however, focusing on learning and providing ourselves with corrective feedback and then concentrating on self-rewards for our desirable behavior will be more effective.

AN EXAMPLE OF SELF-LEADERSHIP IN ACTION

We have observed action-oriented self-leadership strategies being used in a variety of work settings. Knowledge-based work settings that rely heavily on information technology involve a number of substantial challenges for self-leadership. People can find themselves spending much time on their own staring at computer screens and trying to find motivation within themselves. The days when people called "bosses" closely monitored and directed other people referred to as "subordinates" are quickly fading into the past (we even titled one of our previous books *Business Without Bosses*).

Many self-managing work systems found in today's organizations originally emerged from manufacturing settings rather than electronic-based offices. For example, in one particularly impressive high-performing plant organized according to a self-managed team concept (the system is structured around teams of workers who are largely responsible for managing themselves), we observed countless scribbled notes pasted to machines to serve as self-established cues for guiding workers. (For more details, see the chapter on leading teams.) And workers used other strategies such as self-observation, rehearsal, self-praise, and self-criticism readily within their teams. The following examples illustrate what we observed:

"Hey Frank, you did a hell of a job in cleaning up our work area," Tom shouted with obvious sincerity over the hum of the machines. After giving Frank a quick pat on the back, Tom returned to his work location. He glanced at a note he had stuck to the front of his machine that described the new, more efficient welding procedure that he had helped to develop. After a moment of reflection, he began working again. A couple of hours later, as his team left for lunch, they noticed that the previous month's efficiency ratings were posted on the bulletin board outside the cafeteria. "All right!" shrieked Elizabeth, one of Tom's energetic peers, "we did it! We improved by ten percent!" The group stopped to give one another hearty handshakes, backslaps, and hugs before going in for lunch with their pride apparent in their strides.

Two o'clock that afternoon the team held a special meeting. "You know Bill didn't show up for work again today after being out twice last week," Tom started. "We agreed if it happened one more time we'd have to counsel him. That's why I invited Smitty [Smitty was the team's external leader, though he served more as a coach and counselor than supervisor] to help us practice what we would say to him." Frank played the role of Bill while the rest of the team practiced what it planned to say. Smitty provided feedback and suggestions while the team worked out its plan.

CONCLUSION

In this chapter we focused on action-oriented self-leadership strategies and examples. These strategies are especially useful for enhancing work performance on difficult and often unattractive tasks. Later, we discuss how SuperLeaders can promote employee self-leadership by modeling, encouraging, guiding, and reinforcing use of these kinds of tools. Before we turn to the details of how a Super-Leader might accomplish this, we need to explore additional self-leadership strategies. These additional strategies provide the potential for helping people discover natural motivation in their feelings about their work, and to establish constructive patterns of thinking. More specifically, in the next two chapters we turn to the role of natural rewards that produce self-motivation, and self-leadership of the mind.

Carly Fiorina of Hewlett-Packard

Seokhwa Yun and Henry P. Sims, Jr.

Carly Fiorina was appointed President and Chief Executive Officer (CEO) of Hewlett-Packard (HP) in July 1999. This appointment makes HP the largest public corporation ever to be run by a woman. Fiorina comes to HP with an exceptional track record of accelerating growth in large technology businesses. She has distinguished herself in tough, competitive environments, including AT&T, Lucent Technologies, and now HP. She has been named by *Fortune* magazine as the most powerful woman in American business.

As we enter the 21st century, HP is one of those companies at the cusp of the digital revolution. Fiorina has charged HP to "keep the best, invent the rest."[1] She is challenging HP to transform its culture, speed up product development, and, most of all, to increase the company's Internet-related business. The main direction is moving from a product-oriented company to one focused on e-service solutions. She intends to return HP to its vaunted reputation for innovation, but by concentrating on integrated customer solutions as opposed to pieces of hardware. Through her appointment, the HP board unanimously agreed that she was quite simply the ideal candidate to leverage HP's core strengths into the rapidly changing information-systems industry and to lead this great company into the new millennium.

Fiorina has definitive views on leadership, which she shared with us during a personal interview at the University of Maryland.[2] From our viewpoint, she is an exceedingly complex leader, mixing several of the types of leadership we present here in *The New SuperLeadership*. Fundamentally, we found her personal leadership philosophy to be deeply rooted in the values of SuperLeadership—she believes in empowering others. And, in her determination to change the culture of HP, she clearly demonstrates elements of Visionary Hero leadership with occasional uses of Transactor and Directive leadership.

Carleton (Carly) S. Fiorina[3]

Carly Fiorina is the recently appointed president and CEO of HP Company, which is a leading global provider of computing, Internet and Intranet solutions, services, communications products, and measurement solutions. All of its businesses are recognized for excellence in quality and support. The company headquarters are in Palo Alto, California. She became president and CEO of HP on July 17, 1999, and joined the HP board of directors. Recently named by *Fortune* as the most powerful woman in American business, Ms. Fiorina brings to HP nearly 20 years of broad technology and telecommunications experience at Lucent Technologies and AT&T, and a demonstrated track record of successfully growing large businesses. During her last two years as president of Lucent's Global Service Provider Business, the division dramatically increased its growth rate under her leadership, rapidly expanded its international revenues, and gained market share in every region across every product line. Previously, she had spearheaded the planning and execution of Lucent's 1996 initial public offering (IPO) and subsequent spinoff from AT&T, one of the largest and most successful IPOs ever. Prior to her involvement with Lucent, Ms. Fiorina held a number of senior positions at AT&T.

Ms. Fiorina was born on September 6, 1954, in Austin, Texas. She holds a bachelor's degree in medieval history and philosophy from Stanford University, a master's degree in business administration from the Robert H. Smith School of Business at the University of Maryland at College Park, Md., and a master of science degree from MIT's Sloan School.

Ms. Fiorina is a member of the board of directors of the Kellogg Company and Merck & Co., Inc. She recently was elected to the U.S. China Board of Trade. Previously she held positions on the boards of directors of the USA Republic of China Economic Council; Goldstar Information & Communications, Inc. of Seoul, Korea; and AT&T Taiwan Telecommunications of Taipei. She also served on the board of the Telecommunications Industry Association.

In this profile, we will discuss in detail Fiorina's use of various approaches to leadership. But first, it's clear from our interview with her that she is a highly accomplished self-leader whose control and influence over herself have guided and fueled her remarkable rise to corporate leadership.

LEADING YOURSELF

Self-leadership is the influence we exert over ourselves to control our own behavior and thinking, and especially to enhance our own performance. Fiorina expressed a keen sense of her own self-leadership capability, starting with crediting her parents with imparting some basic values that have influenced her life. "I give my parents great credit. . . . I grew up with [a feeling that has carried over] into my life and my professional career . . . a sense of 'no limitations.' I grew up in a family where my parents made it very clear that I could do anything I wanted to do, and the only limitation that was placed on me was the one I put on myself."

It seems clear that a primary self-motivator for Fiorina is her quest for natural rewards. She has to have a passion for what she does: "For me, the criteria has always been, 'Will I like it?' I mean, 'Will I enjoy doing it? Will I find it interesting?'"

She continued about passion: "I love what I do. Always have. [If] I don't love it, I don't do it any more. It's too hard not to love it. . . . Never sell your soul, because nobody can ever pay it back. . . . You have to have your own center, and have your own sense of what is right and wrong."

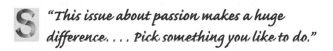

S *"This issue about passion makes a huge difference. . . . Pick something you like to do."*

She has a natural curiosity, and being able to satisfy that curiosity has been an important factor in determining which jobs she would accept—which career choices she would make. "I am always looking for new challenges, something new to learn, and that has caused me to take some changes to my career that served me very well. . . . Some jobs were probably not the best . . . from a classical career trajectory standpoint. But I took them because they were interesting to me and they were challenging to me."

The opportunity to learn is another important criterion that guides her decision-making about herself. "I took jobs I was least prepared for because I was going to learn something. . . . [And] some of the best lessons I have ever learned have been from the worst bosses I have ever had. . . . Learning is an active sport!"

She thinks of life " . . . as a journey. Pause at moments to see life's markers and the patterns that emerge. . . . Engage your whole self in everything you do."[4]

All of these characteristics amply demonstrate Fiorina's capacity as a self-leader. She leads herself to do what she loves to do with passion and professionalism. She pursues challenge, thinks of opportunities, learns from anyone, and loves what she does. Most of all, her philosophy about her own self-leadership provides a road map that guides her leadership of others.

LEADING OTHERS

Visionary Hero

We found it impossible to categorize Fiorina into a single dominant leadership type. She demonstrates behaviors of different types of leadership at different times. As a leader of an organization on the cusp of dramatic cultural change, she certainly qualifies as a Visionary Hero. She walks a fine line between dictating a top-down vision versus a bottom-up approach. She calls this a "loose/tight" approach. "To lead effectively, a leader has to create a context for people. What's the strategic vision? What's the environment we are trying to create? How do we measure success? Then, once that context is created, I delegate a lot and I give people a lot of freedom of movement within that set of parameters."

She readily admits to having her own vision. "People have to know what to expect from you." Her vision for HP revolves around reviving HP's reputation for innovation. To back this up, she has committed a new $200 million advertising campaign, centered on the word "invent."

SuperLeadership

But Fiorina's fundamental view of leadership is quite consistent with the philosophy of SuperLeadership, with its emphasis on the follower rather than the leader: "Remember that leadership is not in fact about you, but about the people who you are trying to inspire by unleashing their talents, their hopes, their aspirations."[5]

She clearly is committed to encouraging independent action by her followers: "Leadership in this new landscape is not about controlling decision-making. We don't have time anymore to control decision-making. It's about creating the right environment, empowerment. It is about setting guidelines and boundaries and parameters and then setting people free."[6]

She continues on the theme of empowerment: "It's about challenging minds and capturing hearts. . . . Strategy is ultimately about people . . . your ultimate job is to let them go."[7] Her philosophy on empowerment has a purpose: "[It] keeps people engaged and interested."

 "Leadership in this new era is about empowering others to decide for themselves . . . and reach their full potential."

Goal Setting

Fiorina is deeply involved in a collaborative goal-setting process with her followers: "We talk about how we measure success. . . . [It can be] financial goals, market share goals, retention goals. But I generally don't tell people how to get it done. I do spend a lot of time getting an agreement on what we are going to get done. The what, not the how."

Listening

Interestingly, of all the various aspects of SuperLeadership Fiorina focuses on listening skills as most important: "I spend four to five hours a month listening to people come in with bright ideas. . . . It has to do with people feeling valued . . . with people feeling as though they really do have an opportunity to speak to the most senior folks of the firm and they will be listened to. . . . Most people not only feel valued when you ask them but they also respect you more for taking the time to think that they might have something that you could learn from. [I say], 'I would really appreciate your help.'"

Encouraging Natural Rewards

She is mindful of her personal feelings about her own curiosity and the importance of doing work she likes when it comes to leading others: "Nonmonetary things can make a huge difference to people. . . . I think fun and enjoyment and having a passion for what you do is a big piece of keeping people going. . . . I think people would say they have fun working with me."

She further states, "If you create an environment where people's hearts and minds are fully engaged, where strategy is ennobling, where great aspirations are powered by the desires of people to do something worthwhile, then you will have touched others you encounter on your journey. . . . Make the choice to do something because it engages your heart as well as your mind."[8]

Encouraging Opportunity Thinking

Fiorina clearly has a perspective that is consistent with the notion of "opportunity thinking" and she intends to pass this mindset on to her followers. In her case, opportunity thinking falls within the sphere of risk-taking, which she believes to be an important part of leadership: "We need people who can handle greater ambiguity and risk."[9]

The way a leader responds to mistakes is an important element in fostering risk-taking, and Fiorina has clear opinions on this topic: "You [have to] realize that you can make mistakes, and to know when you have made them, and admit when you have made them."

S *"You've got to let people make mistakes and survive."*

"I don't shoot somebody the first time they miss, because people do make mistakes. People have to see that there is an opportunity to make a mistake or fail and survive, or what you are doing is running an organization completely on fear. . . . We spend a lot of time on what happened and why did it happen, how would we do it differently next time. That's the coaching part of the job . . . which is important." Of course there are limits: "Mistakes are valuable as long as you don't make the same one over and over again. . . . People miss a number three or four times, then we [have] a different conversation."

Transactor and Directive Leadership

Finally, it's important to note that at times Fiorina can act as a Directive or Transactor leader. In the past, executive pay at HP was measured against internal goals. Today, compensation is much more contingent upon external comparisons, including the performance of HP stock. Her new pay plan rewards aggressive risk-takers.

She is not shy about asserting her authority: "It is important for people to have an opportunity to be heard. But it also has to be clear who gets to decide what, and it then needs to be clear when discussion is over."[10] Previously, the convention at consensus-driven HP was that any manager could exercise a veto by saying "no." Fiorina has occasionally responded to veto attempts: "I make the decisions now."[11]

LEADERSHIP FOR THE FUTURE

Fiorina's entry seems to have caused quite a stir at HP. While much of her leadership is focused on relatively short-term organizational change, she clearly has her eye on the long run: "After three years, people [will] know that there is an environment that is receptive to different ideas and different approaches [based on] either a technology breakthrough or a market fact. We are doing more and more around connecting technology to the market, earlier and earlier."

She seems totally conscious of the importance of her leadership at this particular moment in time. She speaks of leadership as "performance" and seems keenly aware of prominence and visibility. She seems to have deliberately tied HP's march into the new millennium to her own energetic nature and media fame: "*You* do it. If you don't walk the walk, nothing will matter to the contrary."[12]

Although her leadership is indeed complex, blending elements of Visionary Hero, Transactor, and Strongman leadership, her heart seems to be firmly rooted in the tenets of SuperLeadership: "Every man and every woman on this earth is born to lead. A leader's greatest obligation is to make possible an environment where people's minds and hearts can be inventive, brave ... where people can aspire to change the world."[13]

Perhaps most of all, her own self-motivation to accomplish great things is captured by this deeply introspective statement: "I love ... seeing people and seeing organizations do more than they thought they were capable of. I just love to see it." Carly Fiorina is undoubtedly on a mission to lead venerable HP into the new millennium with an attitude of "doing more than [we were] thought capable of."

5 Self-Leadership Through Natural Rewards

"**Y**OU SURE SEEM TO WORK HARD at your new job, Bill. You must have really received a big pay increase when you took the position."

"Oh, a little one, Frank, but actually I don't make much more than I did in my old position. It's really a lateral move."

"Really? That seems hard to believe. You seem to be more interested and engaged in your work. Why did you take the job?"

"It's kind of hard to explain. It's just that I really like the kind of work I'm doing. When I stopped to think about it, I realized I didn't really need more money to make the decision. I guess I'm getting a kick out of the work itself. I feel effective in what I'm doing and I have more freedom to do the work the way I want. When something gets done I know I've really made a contribution. I'm just plain motivated to do the work for its own value. Don't tell anybody, Frank," Bill said, with a playful smile on his face. "But I probably would do this job even if they paid me less than my old job. One thing is clear, I know my level of performance has really improved with this new job."

How do you feel about your job? Are you putting your time in mainly because of pay? Or, like Bill, does your work provide you with some sense of fulfillment? The basic theme of this chapter is actually rather simple: We believe that people are likely to do a better job if they like the work they do. That is, an important part of self-leadership is to take advantage of the potential natural rewards that derive from the work itself. How can you enhance these natural rewards as a part of your own work and life?

Until very recently, work has been seen as something unpleasant, something secondary to other parts of life. For many even today, work is experienced as something meaningless. Benjamin Hunnicutt, a historian at the University of Iowa says that "Job satisfaction studies over the past 20 years indicate that people are looking for identity, purpose, and meaning in their work, but very few are finding these things."[1] He disparages the traditional motivations to work: "If you work for goals that are only found in the marketplace to improve your reputation or to make more money, for instance—you will not give of yourself freely." Indeed, natural rewards are a critical part of developing one's own self-leadership. The question is, how do we get these natural rewards?

S *Work can provide a set of natural rewards, and these rewards can be highly motivating toward achievement and performance.*

In this chapter we examine how to use natural rewards that derive from the task itself, and the surrounding context, to generate constructive thinking and feeling about our own efforts. We focus on how a person can recognize and enhance natural rewards that come from the task itself, as well as natural rewards that stem from the immediate context or environment surrounding the work. This is particularly important in the information age, when many find themselves spending more time by themselves at their computers or interfacing with depersonalized network technology. Even when people work on teams, more and more these are virtual teams where members communicate through technology such as e-mail rather than face-to-face interaction. All this can eliminate some of the traditional motivations surrounding work. Many have said over the years, "The job is lousy but I enjoy the people." Now the enjoyment often has to come from somewhere else. We believe this makes finding and building natural rewards into work more crucial than ever.

"The nature of work is changing. People are hungry for work that's challenging, exciting, and meaningful."

—Chuck Salter[2]

It used to be that people could depend on each other for motivation and interest through various one-on-one conversations and meetings. But the 21st century is a new era of increased independence from people, while the interdependence is with technology. The personal motivation has to come from within. Self-leadership based on natural rewards is essential if we want our work to be meaningful and motivating in the information age.

The importance of this issue has become even more apparent with the younger workers as we move into the 21st century. The new generation entering the workforce has never seen an economic downturn. They would rather not work than take a job they find unpleasant. More than ever, people are seeking some sort of fulfillment from the work itself.

BUILDING NATURAL REWARDS INTO TASKS

Work, even the seemingly most monotonous kind, has at least some latitude for us to redefine our tasks so that we can enjoy a more positive mental state and feelings. Consider Charlene, the toll booth ticket taker—a job most of us would consider boring to the extreme. She makes a game out of her work each day by attempting to see how many people she can get to smile. One approach to work is mere compliance to the task, just getting the job done. However, most work can be enjoyed to at least some degree and can be performed with commitment, not just compliance, by seeking out and facilitating the natural rewards of tasks.

 Effective self-leadership involves seeking out and facilitating the natural rewards of the task itself.

WHAT ARE NATURAL REWARDS?

As implied by the discussion thus far, an important distinction can be made between two basic types of rewards. The most obvious kind is the external reward, such as a pay raise, time off, vacation, a promotion, an award, a bonus, and so on. Even praise is a form of external reward. These external rewards are important but there is also a second type of reward, generally less recognized and less understood but certainly no less important. We call it a *natural reward*.[3] It is so closely tied to a given task or activity that the two cannot be separated. For example, an individual who enjoys reading the newspaper or going to the theater is usually engaging in an activity that could be described as naturally rewarding. No external incentives are required to motivate this behavior. The incentives are natural; they are built into the task itself. An avid golfer playing golf on Saturday morning is another example. The natural reward comes from the game itself.

 A natural reward ... is so closely tied to a given task or activity that the two cannot be separated.

Steven Jobs of Apple Computer apparently places a very high value on natural rewards. Upon returning to the helm as CEO of Apple in 1997 after an extended leave of over a decade, Jobs refused any pay or stock, instead receiving a token $1 annual salary. In a recent interview Jobs commented, "I didn't return to Apple to make a fortune." He went on to explain that he was lucky enough to become wealthy at a very young age. But, he added, "I don't view wealth as something that validates my intelligence. I just wanted to see if we could work together to turn this thing around when the company was literally on the verge of bankruptcy. The decision to go without pay has served me well."[4] For Jobs, the challenge itself is an important type of natural reward.

WHY ARE SOME ACTIVITIES
NATURALLY REWARDING?

Work is more naturally rewarding when the task delivers three basic elements: a sense of (1) competence, (2) self-control, and (3) purpose. Motivation tends to increase when work is designed in such a way that enhances these feelings and thoughts.

Feelings of Competence

One common aspect of naturally rewarding activities is that they make a person feel more competent. We tend to like a task that we perform well. A couple of good golf shots on the last hole can entice someone to play again.

Of course, activities that enhance feelings of competence are sometimes also tied to external rewards. But the natural rewards built into the task can be a potent motivating force in themselves. The feeling of being competent, and perhaps even the best at something, can be powerfully rewarding even if no praise and material rewards are received. This feeling is important whether the employee is a top executive or an hourly worker.

Consider the example of using your own personal computer. Despite the many technological advances over recent decades, many highly educated people continue to be frustrated by the struggle to get their computers to do what they want them to do. How many times have we had the system just freeze for no apparent cause? This can lead to a painful sense of incompetence, all too often resulting in the declaration, "I guess I'm just technologically challenged."

Interestingly, Steven Jobs, whom we have described as valuing natural rewards personally, seems to view part of Apple Computer's mission and competitive advantage to be its ability to make computers user friendly for consumers. A recent effort at Apple under Job's direct guidance has been the design of a new, more appealing and effortless operating system. The system has been designed to allow users who want to develop new programs to be able to do so more efficiently in "about a tenth the time it would take to write them . . . for any other operating system." In addition, Apple is providing a variety of tools that will allow users to do things like construct and modify Web sites quickly and easily, and to use online data storage space that acts and looks as though it's a local file right inside the computer. The interface between computer and Internet will appear more seamless. If these efforts work out as planned, all this should translate into Apple users being more naturally motivated to use their computers as they work with an enhanced sense of mastery and competence.[5]

Feelings of Self-Control

A second characteristic of naturally enjoyable activities is that they make individuals feel more self-control. Most people have a natural tendency to want to control their own destinies. They seek some feeling of independence and a chance to express their own ideas and creativity. Indeed, we believe this desire is a potent motivation that leads many people to change their careers, including opening their own businesses or undertaking advanced education.

Henry had finished the first round of the decision analysis. He was using a formal decision-making technique that he had found on the Internet to compare the outcomes of continuing his present career with the prospects of returning to school for a Ph.D. and the life of an academic. He was currently a junior manager at a major *Fortune* 500 company and he knew that his potential for promotion and advancement was good.

Henry looked at the analysis, which mainly compared "outcomes" or rewards that stemmed from the two career alternatives. In his first pass, the analysis had come out about even, but Henry was uncomfortable—he thought the analysis was missing something.

Then a thought occurred: "I really haven't considered the control that I have over my day-to-day activities when I compare the two careers." He defined a new career outcome—"the opportunity to choose my own activities"—and recomputed the analysis.

The differences between the two career alternatives became clearer. On the one hand, continuing his path along the executive fast track would provide more money, probably more security, and certainly more stability over the next few years. On the other hand, the academic career track offered an opportunity to work on tasks that he defined for himself—the type of tasks that he really enjoyed.

As Henry looked at the analysis, he knew the next few years were indeed going to be challenging. But he wanted that sense of control. He started to write the letters requesting graduate school applications.

The combination of the desires to feel competent and self-controlling can lead to an interesting pattern—searching for challenges that we are capable of mastering and then actually expending the effort to master them. Cutting a stroke off in a round of golf, or achieving a reasonable increase in performance at work, reflects this kind of pattern. Grappling with reasonable challenges can be naturally rewarding because successfully meeting them can contribute to feelings of competence and self-control.

Feelings of Purpose

Even if a task makes us feel more competent and more self-controlling, it still may not be naturally enjoyable if we don't believe it's worthwhile. People yearn for purpose and meaning.

Consider the case of Michael Marvin, who began his working career as a cigarette salesman. Mike liked the freedom of his job, and in fact it paid quite well. But he was troubled by the ethical questions surrounding his work. "Is it really right to promote this product when the health considerations are so clear?" Mike was a salesperson who was obviously competent, who had freely chosen his job, and who was relatively self-controlling. Still, he did not enjoy his work because of the ethical doubts about what he was doing. It wasn't too long before Mike changed his job. (This is a true story; today Mike is the vice president of marketing in a major manufacturing company.)

Most of the gurus who describe the changing nature of work agree on some basic points: people do their best when they're motivated by a sense of purpose.[6]

But where do feelings of purpose and meaning come from? Many experts would argue that helping or expressing goodwill toward others provides a sense of purpose. In his classic early writings on human stress, Dr. Hans Selye has suggested that the best way to enjoy a rewarding lifestyle free of disabling stress is to practice what he calls "altruistic egoism."[7] In essence, this involves helping others while also recognizing our own needs and enhancing ourselves as individuals (egoism). The philosophy suggests that individuals can only enjoy a happy, meaningful life when they marry their innate self-centered nature as human beings with altruistic efforts that tend to win the goodwill and respect of others.

Regardless of how altruism potentially adds purpose to a task or, more generally, to life, it should not be overlooked. It may be the key to achieving feelings of purpose and meaning.

Tasks that enhance our feelings of competence, self-control, and purpose can provide potent natural rewards.

SELF-REDESIGN OF TASKS

It's easy to have the feeling that we are "stuck" in a job we really don't care for. But to at least some degree it is possible for many of us to redesign our own work. Often we fall into the trap of thinking the design of our work is something unchangeable—a decision by higher management. However, we believe it is possible to enhance our own self-leadership by building more naturally enjoyable features into our tasks. As an example, consider Karen, who has an exceptional ability to redesign her own job.

When Karen reported for work as the new office receptionist, she brought with her qualifications and abilities well beyond her narrow job description. And over a period of weeks and months, through her own initiative, her job changed dramatically until she had become a professional writer and assistant project director for a major project in the firm. She accomplished all this step by step, by taking initiative and tackling challenges outside of her normal job responsibilities. She carefully identified and voluntarily pursued specific opportunities where help was needed. She would ask "May I help you to _____?"

When she began, Karen was given instruction on how to use her computer to do the scheduling and communication that was necessary for her receptionist job. But she quickly found that the computer also had a new word processing program, spreadsheet and database programs, and a routine to simplify project scheduling. She discovered she could communicate with others throughout the office through the company Intranet. She quickly became adept at switching back and forth from her receptionist work to working on the more complex programs. Of course, she was careful to make sure she fulfilled her basic responsibilities as a receptionist.

Gradually, the managers began to realize that Karen could be depended on to undertake and accomplish tasks that were "falling between the cracks." And most of all, she did not act like a receptionist but more like a key organizational employee ready to do whatever needed to be done. As Karen later explained, "I simply redesigned my own job."

Through hard work and initiative, she had taken it upon herself to change her own work and thus provide herself with opportunities for feelings of competence, self-control, and purpose. It wasn't too long before Karen's title, salary, and official responsibilities changed to reflect what she was actually doing. She knew the transition was complete when a new receptionist was hired.

Part of self-leadership involves identifying aspects of tasks that are naturally enjoyable and trying to increase this part of the work as much as is reasonably possible. Karen's case admittedly is a bit extreme, in that she essentially created a new position for herself.

Clearly, there are limitations on how far people can redesign their own jobs. We suggest both a short-run perspective and a long-run perspective. In the short run, the focus is on our present work: How can we make the task itself more naturally rewarding? Essentially, this is the task redesign problem and involves changing what we do and the way we do it. Like Karen, many of us can enhance our own self-leadership by redesigning our own work. On a day-by-day basis, one effective approach is to look for the simple, small next step of doing something in a more enjoyable way.

On the other hand, it's sometimes useful to take more of a long-run perspective. That is, how can we change the nature of our work over a period of years to become more rewarding? As one example, this perspective might lead to a decision to seek more education. And on occasion it might even be necessary to implement the ultimate self-generated job redesign—resigning and leaving our present job and going to work somewhere else. Whether it's short term or long term, an important part of learning to lead ourselves is to be on the lookout for ways to enhance the natural rewards of the task itself. Step by step, it is possible to build more self-leadership into our work by seeking out naturally rewarding tasks that provide feelings of competence, self-control, and purpose.

Another way to find natural rewards centers on the way we think while we perform tasks. We can, for example, think about, talk about, and in general focus on the parts of work that we dislike, inevitably leading to negative feelings about our work. Or we can focus on the rewards expected for performing work (such as money, praise, recognition, and so on) and thus be motivated by images of the future. As a third option, we can focus on the naturally enjoyable aspects of our work and enjoy the activity for whatever immediate value it might have: we can choose to "smell the roses." This last focus is the key to establishing natural enjoyment and being naturally motivated to higher performance.

FINDING NATURAL REWARDS AROUND US

Another approach to finding natural rewards is to consider the context surrounding the work. By "context" we mean the immediate physical environment surrounding our work. Our basic thesis is that our work can be more productive if we do it at a place and time that supports and enhances our efforts. As one example, a business meeting normally held in a stuffy conference room might take on a quite different flavor if the physical surroundings are changed. Consider the case of Sally, who believes there is considerable value in occasionally getting her staff out of the office to talk to each other in a different context.

Sally had always been athletic—she was a star field-hockey player in high school and college. After graduation, she gradually switched to tennis and sailing as her preferred outdoor activities. With her present position as vice president she could afford a nice boat, and had become quite competent as the captain of a 42-foot sailboat that she kept on Long Island Sound.

Sally wanted to get her staff out of the office for a meeting to build some cohesion and to generate some innovative ideas for next year's plan. After some thought, she invited the staff, all eleven of them, out for a day on the Sound.

The day began with Sally as captain sailing the group to Rock Island, a park about an hour's sail off the coast. She had identified a few experienced hands to help sail the boat.

After arriving at Rock Island, the group broke into some smaller working teams to develop ideas for the plan. After a catered lunch, the group came back together for an hour or so to share the results. Sally was delighted with the ideas that emerged. Clearly the day had unshackled their thinking, and she could see the cohesion of the group building. The finale to the day was a "best time" sailing race over a marked course, between two teams that were selected from the staff.

When Sally arrived at the office the next day she could sense the revived enthusiasm of the staff and the new informal communication links that had been established during the staff outing. They were still talking about the race. "Yes," she thought, "getting out of the office was the right thing to do."

Even the timing or scheduling of work can be important. Can we find a different time or place that would be more conducive to our work? For example, some people are "night people" while others are "morning people." One of the authors does about 90 percent of his productive writing in the morning and tries to schedule face-to-face meetings in the afternoon. The degree to which employees can schedule work to fit their own physiological rhythms and psychological preferences will enhance their personal productivity.

 Work is what you want, where you want.
Because work is what you do, not who you are.[8]

CONCLUSION

Some readers may recognize that this discussion of self-designed tasks is fundamentally based on earlier theory and research on intrinsic motivation and enriched job characteristics. A major difference we propose here is that we should recognize and embrace our own responsibility in seeking out the naturally occurring rewards that stem from the task itself. Many believe that the design of their work is a "given," or that it's someone else's responsibility. In contrast, we believe that everyone, if only in minor ways "at the margin," typically can find opportunities to redesign their own tasks.

Perhaps the biggest influence on the nature of work in decades has been the emergence of the Internet. Not surprisingly, given his apparent appreciation of natural rewards, *Fortune* magazine recently proclaimed on its cover about Steven Jobs that, "Now he's out to make the Net more fun."[9] Today, each of us struggles in our quest for how we can use this new technology to be more effective and bring more enjoyment to our work. Some find surfing the Web to be naturally rewarding, while others find it to be a drag. Do you find this new technology naturally rewarding or not? We sincerely wish you and your associates plenty of fun as you find ways of using natural rewards on the road to personal effectiveness.

S *"... The most powerful rewards [are] non-financial— recognition, the opportunity to participate and be challenged, and the sense of doing important work."*

—Steven Kerr[10]

In summary, both short-term and long-term strategies are available for making work more naturally rewarding. These include (1) building natural rewards into the task itself by choosing what we do or how we do it, and (2) choosing a more desirable work context. If we seriously reexamine our own work—what we do, how we do it, and when and where we do it—we can bring a spirit of natural enjoyment and even playfulness to our daily work life by enhancing the naturally rewarding aspects of our work. Most of all, by finding the natural rewards in our work we can make self-leadership a critical part of achieving personal effectiveness.

6 Self-Leadership of the Mind

"NOT AGAIN!" Deborah moaned in an exasperated tone. "Every time I try to make progress on my work I run into some kind of obstacle that blocks my progress. Sometimes I feel like just giving up! This time we have received information from our latest survey indicating that people don't particularly like our customer service program, and the VP has indicated he would like us to make some changes. We've used that program for years and never really had any major problems with it. Why does this have to come up now, right when we are getting ready to launch our new Internet product line!?"

"Actually, Deborah, I have felt that our customer service policies are dated. I've been hoping that we would make some changes for some time now," responded Sarah. "You may recall that I brought this up in a couple of our department meetings but wasn't able to get much support from the rest of the group because we always had too many other irons in the fire. Now maybe this will finally receive some priority. Our new products have been pretty innovative but we have been hindering ourselves with poor customer service. This survey data provides a real opportunity to bring our customer service up to the level of our innovative e-product line."

This story is about finding an opportunity within what first seems to be an obstacle. How do you respond when faced with challenges? Do you find yourself becoming frustrated and trying to avoid these situations as much as possible? Or, do you often find that your best innovation is stimulated by confronting challenges? Are you a "Sarah" who looks at an obstacle and tries to see the opportunities that lie ahead?

Self-leadership of the mind is mainly concerned with the process of how individuals constructively manage patterns of thinking, which in turn influences action. Just as we develop habits in our behavior, we also develop habits in our thoughts, such as a tendency to dwell on opportunities or obstacles. The challenge is to manage our thought patterns in such a way that we increase our personal effectiveness in our work and life. In this chapter, we discuss cognitive approaches to self-leadership that include managing our own beliefs, imagined experiences, and self-talk.

 "The mind is its own place, and in itself can make a Heaven of Hell, a Hell of Heaven."

—**John Milton**

Bill Gates provided a good example of effective management of thought patterns when he discussed how to accept bad news in his book, *Bill Gates @ the Speed of Thought*. "Once you embrace unpleasant news not as negative but as evidence of a need for change," he says, "you aren't defeated by it. You're learning from it."[1] He then goes on to list many costly Microsoft failures that later provided opportunities for the development of many of Microsoft's biggest successes. For example, many "wasted" years working on a failed database called Omega resulted in the most popular desktop database, Microsoft Access. Millions of dollars and countless hours invested in a joint operating system project with IBM, which was discontinued, led to the operating system Windows NT. And a failed Multiplan spreadsheet that made little headway against Lotus 1-2-3 provided learning that helped in the development of Microsoft Excel, an advanced graphical spreadsheet that now leads the competition. Clearly, Bill Gates chose a pattern of thinking that has helped him and his company to turn potential failures into dynamic successes.

*"The great man presides over all his
states of consciousness with obstinate rigor."*

—Leonardo Da Vinci[2]

CHANGING THE WAY WE THINK

Influencing our own thought patterns is no easy task. In fact, a major issue in the field of psychology is how to deal with something (thoughts) that can't be seen or fully understood. Indeed, telling oneself to "think differently" or trying to change patterns of thought through force of will is generally not very productive. On the other hand, some tools (some levers to pull) can facilitate this objective. Specifically they include managing beliefs, imagined experience, and self-talk.

 *Just as we develop habits in our behavior,
we develop habitual patterns of thinking.*

Beliefs

Dr. Albert Ellis, a leading expert on self-improvement therapy, maintains that beliefs can serve as a basis for change.[3] According to the underlying theory, when a person has difficulty coping with certain situations this ineffectiveness can often be traced to irrational beliefs—for example, a fear of speaking stemming from a belief that listeners will respond with rejection. This is a form of obstacle thinking. Obstacle thinking is typically driven by fear, especially fear of failure. Only by challenging these dysfunctional beliefs, so the reasoning goes, can a person successfully deal with the problem. Ideally, thought patterns are established that are centered on opportunities—opportunity thinking—rather than obstacles. Opportunity thinking can offer some significant advantages, since it can lead to greater creativity, innovation, and the positive risk-taking that is so crucial in this fast-paced information age.

"The greatest mistake you can make in life is to be continually fearing you will make one."

—**Elbert Hubbard**[4]

One of the most important beliefs that influences our self-leadership capability is our view of our own ability to carry out a task. Do I really believe I can do it? This belief is called self-efficacy. Research shows that our self-efficacy beliefs become self-fulfilling prophecies; that is, positive beliefs about our ability to perform successfully enhances the probability of actually *doing* it. Conversely, negative beliefs decrease the probability. Our state of mind about ourselves clearly has an impact on ultimate performance. Consider the case of Bonnie Dunbar, whose belief in herself was a critical element in her persistent effort to become a NASA astronaut.

"I've made good use of my time by remaining optimistic and energetic about the future, and by choosing not to agonize over things that I can't change." Bonnie Dunbar has scaled the pinnacle of career success to her current position of NASA astronaut. This achievement is all the more remarkable given the "no female" policy of NASA at the time Bonnie was growing up.

"I wanted to be an astronaut at a time when there weren't any women astronauts. When I was growing up, women couldn't do what I wanted to do. Yet, I clung to my goal." So Bonnie persisted. First, she studied engineering. Then she was told she was too old to be a pilot. Eventually, she became a mission specialist and payload commander, with responsibility for the scientific projects on shuttle flights. As of this writing, she has flown into space five times.

"I've always believed that if you remain optimistic, and if you prepare yourself for opportunities, then those opportunities will find you."[5]

Purposefully changing beliefs is a difficult process. Beliefs are often so ingrained into our personality that we have a difficult time even recognizing them and the way they influence our actions. As a result, purposely identifying and challenging our own dysfunctional beliefs is a useful first step.

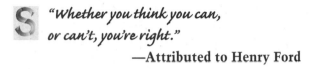

*"Whether you think you can,
or can't, you're right."*
—**Attributed to Henry Ford**

Some might attribute the divergent ways in which people view their jobs to fundamental personality differences and thus consider them beyond influence. However, we think such an interpretation is too simplistic. While personalities can be important, self-leadership enables us to influence how we think about our jobs as well as our more general patterns of thinking and behavior.

Imagined Experience

We carry unique worlds around in our heads. An especially vivid form of these psychological worlds consists of imagined experiences. These images occur naturally and can have either a constructive or destructive influence. Imagining a klutzy performance and utter embarrassment in front of others in a first attempt at some activity (water skiing, golf, speaking in front of a group, and so on) can undermine our confidence, detract from our enjoyment, and ultimately contribute to the very failure we feared.

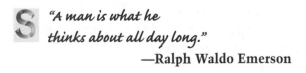

*"A man is what he
thinks about all day long."*
—**Ralph Waldo Emerson**

We can, however, challenge our mental habits by purposefully choosing to form constructive mental images. We can create vivid mental images in our mind, e.g., of dramatic success in the face of major challenges in our work. Similarly, we can rehearse an activity in our mind, or use our imagination to challenge those destructive imagined experiences that enter our psychological world. Again, this is no easy task, but it is possible to establish these positive thought patterns. Over time we can use mental images to introduce positive changes. Consider the following incident, based on an interview that took place on a TV sports-news program:

A high-jump star had just broken the world high-jump record. This performance was especially remarkable given that his own height was only about five feet eight inches, but he had high-jumped over seven and one-half feet. "What do you think about just before you make your jump?" asked the announcer.

"Well," replied the young star, "I have this picture of myself in my mind...just floating over the bar. When I can get this image fixed in my mind, I know I can make the jump."

In sports, imagined experience is called "visualization" and consists of a deliberate attempt to see successful performance of a sports event in one's own "mind's eye." Research has shown that visualization can indeed enhance actual sports performance, and encouraging this strategy has now become a widespread coaching technique. Visualization can be similarly applied to work situations to enhance one's own achievements at work. Visualization may be particularly useful the next time you make a speech or deliver a briefing. Try to engage in a mental rehearsal by visualizing yourself delivering the speech in a very effective manner.

Self-Talk
Though we may deny it, we do talk to ourselves. Usually these conversations take place at an internal, unobservable level. The per-

son that botches a work assignment and finds herself engaging in internal self-critical speech—"You dummy! Why did you do that? Can't you get anything right?" is a representative example. Of course it's easy to recognize that this kind of internal verbal abuse is not going to provide much benefit. Instead, a more constructive, analytic approach—"What went wrong? I know I can do better than that. What can I do to improve my performance next time?"—is likely to reap more positive benefits.

S *Perhaps it's time you had a talk with yourself.*

Most people are very careful about how they talk to others, especially in sensitive situations. Unfortunately, they are usually much less considerate of what they say to themselves. They rarely think about self-conversations nor do they consider the possibility of changing them. Self-observation of patterns of internal dialogue and efforts to replace dysfunctional with constructive self-statements are useful ways to help effectively manage thinking. Perhaps it's time you had a talk with yourself on this subject. We doubt you'll find anywhere a better listener, or one that could benefit more from what you have to say.

MANAGING THOUGHT PATTERNS AND EMOTIONAL INTELLIGENCE

Substantial research concludes that patterns of thinking can influence health, longevity, success, and many other aspects of life. Some of this research is a refinement of earlier work on self-fulfilling prophecies.

According to Dr. Martin Seligman, a leading researcher in this area: "My hunch is that for a given level of intelligence your actual achievement is a function not just of talent, but also of the capacity to stand defeat."[6] For example, in a study of insurance agents Seligman found that the manner in which agents dealt with failures often directly influenced whether they became outstanding salespersons or quit the company. Agents with an optimistic outlook sold 37 percent more insurance in their first two years than agents with pessimistic views. Furthermore, pessimists were twice as likely to quit in their first year. What seems to be important is whether an individual will keep going when things get frustrating.

 "Our expectancies not only affect how we see reality but also affect the reality itself."

—Edward E. Jones[7]

More recently, significant attention has been focused on the concept of emotional intelligence, or the emotional quotient (symbolized by the letters EQ), made popular by the author Daniel Goleman in his book *Emotional Intelligence.*[8] Research in this area suggests that a person's EQ can be as important as IQ (Intelligence Quotient) for determining effectiveness and success. Among other strengths, people with higher EQ tend to be more perceptive of hidden opportunities and interpersonal challenges that need to be addressed. By tapping into our emotional energy and our intuition, emotional intelligence can allow us to move beyond any capacity that is based on only rational and intellectual intelligence. Part of the challenge is to see our emotions as sources of useful information and even wisdom as opposed to a distracting intrusion. Since our emotions are highly interconnected with our thoughts, effectively managing our thought patterns is key.

We suggest a simple exercise to help you gain some insight about your own patterns of thinking. First, divide a piece of paper into two columns. Then identify a disturbing situation that seems to negatively affect your thinking and emotions. Next, list your dysfunctional thoughts about the situation in one column and list alternate, more constructive thoughts in the other. Then ask yourself: What can you do to turn the disagreeable into something that you can use in a constructive way?

Consider the case of Morten Lingelem—farmer and executive with Norsk Hydro, the Norwegian energy and food company.[9]

Morten lives at his ancestral farm, located about 90 minutes by train outside Oslo. His is an active farm, and while it doesn't make a lot of money it seems to satisfy an emotional connection that Morten has to the land.

But Morten is also an engineering manager with Norsk Hydro, and his main office is located within Oslo. Every weekday, shortly after 6 A.M., Morton boards a train near his home for the 90-minute ride into Oslo. He has a standing reservation in the train's "office car," where he can work on his laptop in quiet comfort. Morten has turned an obstacle (the 180-minute commute) into an opportunity—he wonders how he ever got along without the solitary "desk time" that he gets on the train each day.

 "Our problems do not lie in what we experience, but in the attitude we have towards it."

—**Akong Rimpoche**[10]

Earlier in the chapter we shared some of Bill Gates' thoughts on the importance of turning failures into successes. Interestingly, some of his comments on the challenge of managing thinking in the face of difficulties fit well with the topic of Emotional Intelligence. "It's all in how you approach failures. And believe me, we know a lot about failures at Microsoft. . . . The weight of all of our failures could make me too depressed to come in to work. Instead, I am excited about the challenges and by how we can use today's bad news to help solve tomorrow's problems."[11] After studying these thoughts we couldn't help wondering if Bill Gates' tremendous run of success stems largely from his emotional intelligence, especially in the area of dealing with potential failures, which enables him to continually adjust and learn as he goes.

ON LEADING YOURSELF

While a dramatic shift away from traditional management methods has been taking place over the past few decades, leadership is still primarily viewed as an external and usually top-down process. Organizations are still seeking ways to tap into the full potential of their human capital. Despite this desire, one of the primary continuing weaknesses of contemporary organizations is the neglect of the self-leadership capability of people. The capability of people to lead themselves may be the greatest remaining untapped natural resource in the world today.

 Our state of mind about ourselves has a clear impact on ultimate performance.

SuperLeadership can help people learn and effectively practice self-leadership. But first, a SuperLeader must recognize what self-leadership is all about. The specific self-leadership strategies presented in these last three chapters are summarized in the chart on the next page.

By mastering action-oriented self-leadership strategies such as self-set goals and self-rewards, people can work through difficult and sometimes unattractive tasks. Furthermore, by building in the natural rewards of work that promote feelings of competence, self-control, and purpose, people can motivate themselves to achieve higher performance through natural enjoyment. Finally, the establishment of effective thought patterns through the self-management of beliefs, imagined experience, and self-talk can contribute to overall effectiveness. By modeling, encouraging, reinforcing, and otherwise facilitating these self-leadership processes in others, a leader can become a SuperLeader.

ACTION-ORIENTED SELF-LEADERSHIP STRATEGIES

Strategy

Self-Set Goals	Setting goals for your own work efforts.
Management of Cues	Arranging and altering cues in the work environment to facilitate your desired personal behaviors.
Rehearsal	Physical or mental practice of work activities before you actually perform them.
Self-Observation	Observing and gathering information about your own specific behaviors that you have targeted.
Self-Reward	Providing yourself with personally valued rewards for completing desirable behaviors.
Self-Punishment	Administering punishments to yourself for behaving in undesirable ways. (While this strategy is generally *not* very effective, constructive self-correcting feedback can be.)

SELF-LEADERSHIP THROUGH NATURAL REWARDS

Self-Redesign of Tasks	Self-redesign of what you do and how you do your work to increase the level of natural rewards In your Job. Natural rewards that are part of, rather than separate from, the task itself (i.e., the work, like a hobby, becomes the reward) result from activities that cause you to feel: ▶ a sense of competence ▶ a sense of self-control ▶ a sense of purpose
Redesign of the Context of Your Work	Redesigning the immediate surroundings of your work or changing the time and place of your work to enhance the natural rewards that stem from this immediate environment.

SELF-LEADERSHIP OF THE MIND

Establishing Constructive Thought Patterns	Establishing constructive and effective habits or patterns in your thinking (e.g., a tendency to search for opportunities rather than obstacles embedded in challenges) by managing your: ▶ beliefs and assumptions ▶ mental imagery ▶ internal self-talk

The human capacity for self-leadership may be the greatest remaining untapped natural resource in the world today.

By learning self-leadership skills, people bring new meaning to the term "follower." A follower who is self-led is one who brings great capacity to exercise initiative, creativity, and discretion over his or her own work. We are turning the traditional definition of "follower" upside down. Today's followers are really adept leaders of themselves. Self-leadership lies at the crux of how we manage information and knowledge to meet our personal and organizational goals.

The management of information and knowledge is the key to success in the 21st century. Employees cannot accomplish this task blindly, passively dependent on the close direction of traditional leaders. Instead, they must be well armed with an extensive repertoire of self-leadership skills to enable them to react and adjust to an ever-changing environment that is rich with information. Most of all, SuperLeaders can help others to build their own self-leadership.

SuperLeadership in the Information Age—Leading By Creating Knowledge Self-Leaders[1]

Vikas Anand and Don Harrison

As organizations enter the bold new world of the 21st century they are faced with multiple challenges. Foremost among these challenges is the need to better manage knowledge and information. Indeed, Peter Drucker has pointed out that firms that fall to effectively harness their knowledge are doomed to mediocrity or even failure. In this context, we believe that SuperLeadship provides a novel and effective approach to managing knowledge. While leadership is typically associated with individuals, the knowledge management approach defined below is an example of leadership expressed at the level of the organization, where an entire firm, through its systems, practices, and procedures, acts as a SuperLeader.

CHARACTERISTICS OF KNOWLEDGE-INTENSIVE ENVIRONMENTS

As an organization prepares to face the 21st century, it is confronted with a major challenge. One of its key resources—knowledge—is held in the minds of its various employees and scattered all over the organization. Collectively the organization may know a great deal; yet often, employees find that they personally possess inadequate or inappropriate knowledge. The knowledge they need may be known by someone thousands of miles away; obtaining such knowledge in quick time poses a significant challenge. As Dick Loehr, director of Ernst & Young's Center for Business Knowledge points out, such problems can be addressed by implementing a knowledge management system that allows people to "interact, communicate, collaborate, and share information, no matter where they [are]."

THE SUPERLEADERSHIP APPROACH
TO KNOWLEDGE MANAGEMENT

A SuperLeadership approach to knowledge management involves the implementation of a system that values each individual employee and aims to make each a knowledge leader. The system creates an environment that facilitates employees in their efforts to practice knowledge self-leadership, builds natural rewards into the knowledge management process, and helps employees in the field to act and make key decisions without supervision from their bosses.

Developing Knowledge Self-Leaders

One approach to managing knowledge involves the nurturing of experts in specific areas. When adopting such an approach, a firm invests in recruiting and developing key experts in a variety of specific knowledge domains. Employees may have to depend on their relationship with that expert for required knowledge. From a leadership perspective, such an approach creates a few expert leaders who control key organizational activities, and introduces the conditions for controlling (even "Strongman" type) leaders to emerge.

A SuperLeadership approach, on the contrary, values *all* individual employees and develops them into "knowledge leaders" in their own right. Such a firm accumulates the knowledge of various individuals, thoroughly vets it for accuracy, and then enables all employees to tap into this knowledge. Employees are not required to refer to knowledgeable experts for key knowledge; instead, each employee decides what knowledge is required and the firm facilitates her efforts to acquire it. This philosophy becomes a means of creating self-leaders in the organization and helps each employee to act effectively without guidance from superiors.

 SuperLeaders value all individual employees and work to develop them into "knowledge leaders."

Establishing a Nurturing Environment for Knowledge Self-Leaders

A Knowledge-SuperLeadership approach requires the creation of employees who are knowledgeable about some areas, but can easily educate themselves in other areas, by rapidly acquiring expertise available collectively within the firm. This approach can succeed only if employees continuously augment their existing knowledge and are motivated to acquire required expertise; if they are not, even the best knowledge-management technology is likely to fail.

A key step in the knowledge empowerment process involves the conversion of large amounts of tacit knowledge held by various experts (that does not travel freely from one individual to another) into explicit knowledge. This process can be handled in a variety of ways. For instance, Ernst & Young (E&Y) established the Center for Business Knowledge in 1993, and a representative from the Center was assigned to each of 40 distinct areas of expertise to expedite knowledge conversion. Experts in given areas were encouraged to dwell on their experiences, share them with other individuals, and make repeated efforts to document their knowledge. As a result, large volumes of knowledge were recorded and stored electronically on E&Y's Lotus Notes system. Xerox followed a similar process when it developed the Eureka "tips" database for its worldwide service engineers. One of our favorite stories about the conversion of tacit knowledge into explicit is about a Xerox engineer in France who recorded the sound made by a key copier component just before it was heading toward failure. He then loaded the recording as a digital file on the firm's knowledge database, with advice to users to change the relevant part when they heard that particular sound.

 Knowledge within an organization needs to be set up so that it can be efficiently accessed by employees.

Once knowledge has been gathered in an explicit form, it needs to be organized to ensure that employees can tap into it. For instance, Ernst & Young organized the large volumes of its explicit knowledge into "Power-Packs." PowerPacks are electronic encyclopedias of knowledge pertaining to specific areas of expertise. Each PowerPack is a compilation of outstanding proposals, presentations, competitive models, specialized tools, and a variety of other business-related information relevant to a specific industry or area. PowerPacks provide masses of data, and employees can sort through relevant items using sophisticated search engines. Employees from the Center for Business Knowledge regularly check the content of each PowerPack to ensure that their data is relevant and current. Each PowerPack thus serves as an "expert center" that empowers employees with the knowledge they need. In addition to PowerPacks, vast amounts of information were posted on central computers, updated regularly, and made accessible to employees. An Ernst & Young manager stated: "Earlier, it would take me several days to learn of SEC updates . . . now I have them the day they are issued."

 With true SuperLeadership a culture is established that fosters not hoarding but sharing knowledge by all employees.

A SuperLeadership approach to knowledge empowerment also involves the establishment of a knowledge-sharing culture that encourages employees to share rather than to hoard knowledge. Such a culture encourages employees to unhesitatingly seek required knowledge from others. A knowledge-sharing culture can be created in a variety of ways. For instance, in Xerox top management continually exhorted employees to engage in knowledge sharing by explicitly including knowledge sharing as a key desired behavior in their cultural document. Another firm, Damark International, has experimented with a new position—Manager of Relationships—that focuses on developing better interpersonal relationships among employees.

Facilitating Self-Rewards

The process of knowledge-empowering employees is not always smooth. Firms that attempt to knowledge-empower all employees can face unexpected challenges from employees who resist adopting new behaviors. Indeed, many employees may perceive sharing their personal knowledge as a loss of control.

While it may be tempting for firms to use direct monetary rewards to induce knowledge-sharing behaviors, such inducements must be used with caution. A multinational firm that was building a knowledge database announced a scheme that provided monetary rewards to employees who contributed knowledge tips to its database. The scheme, however, backfired as employees flooded the database with vast numbers of rather trivial tips. A better approach would be to build natural rewards into behaviors that facilitate knowledge sharing.

S *Using direct monetary rewards to induce knowledge sharing is tempting but can result in unintended and undesirable consequences.*

For instance, Carmen, a manager in a large multinational firm, has found contributing to her firm's knowledge banks rewarding because of the intrinsic reward she gets in knowing the value of the help she provides to other managers. She described an occasion when she received a call from a manager 2000 miles away: "He was so excited because he used a presentation that I had posted [on the firm's knowledge database] to meet an important deadline.... When I feel lazy about posting stuff, I recall his delight [and that prods me on]."

Natural rewards are best built into a knowledge management system when the process provides employees with increased control and purpose to their work, and increases their belief in their ability to perform their tasks. In this context we find interesting the following "success story" that was posted on the Web pages of Ernst & Young's Center for Business Knowledge:

> It seemed like an impossible request. Our team had just delivered a proposal to evaluate the systems conversion at a large Health Care client. They were ready to give us the go-ahead but their chief technology officer wouldn't sign off until he saw a detailed work plan. Normally, that's the first thing we prepare after the client signs an agreement, because it takes quite a bit of time and effort to put it together.
>
> It was pretty clear ... if we didn't prepare the work plan, we'd lose the client.
>
> We had to work fast and smart. We went straight to the ISAAS V6 PowerPack. We found audit programs from other conversion projects around the country. Using those programs, we quickly put together a detailed task plan that would work for this client. We submitted it to the CTO, he reviewed it and approved it that day.

This illustration provides insights into how E&Y has facilitated employees to build in natural rewards. First, it appears that E&Y provides its employees with *control* of their tasks. They did not have to refer to an expert in the area.

The employees identified the knowledge that they needed for a specific problem. Had the team needed to check with the relevant experts for required knowledge, the deal probably would not have been concluded. Second, the employees can directly perceive the impact of their efforts. For instance, in this incident the consultant was excited because she could directly relate her team's efforts to signing the deal. This provided a strong sense of *purpose* to her task. Finally, as employees find themselves coping with complex tasks successfully, their perceptions of their competence also increase.

CONCLUSIONS

As organizations confront the knowledge-based economies of the 21st century they need to develop systems that unleash the power of their employees. Organizations should believe in their own people, and empower them with knowledge to face the challenges they may encounter in the field. In addition, each individual employee's expertise needs to be valued and tapped to make the firm as a whole more knowledgeable. Creating "knowledge self-leaders" involves building natural rewards into employee tasks. The result can be a highly motivated set of employees who deploy large amounts of knowledge with minimal guidance. This, in effect, would be an *organizational* Super-Leadership approach that can help firms to navigate today's competitive landscape.

Part III

SuperLeadership— It's in the Details

The teacher ... does not bid you enter the house of his wisdom, but rather leads you to the threshold of your own mind.... So must each one of you [develop your own] knowledge and ... [your own] understanding.
—from *The Prophet* by Kahlil Gibran[1]

7 Leading Others to Lead Themselves

THE BOY WATCHED THE MAN CAREFULLY as he walked out of the village. The man was his mother's brother and had watched over the boy since his father had been killed in the raid of the Hill People. More than anything else, the ten-year-old boy wanted to be like the man—to be the best hunter in the village.

Suddenly the man stopped and gazed for a long moment at the boy. Without saying a word he motioned, and the boy knew he meant, "Come with me." With tremendous excitement, the boy followed the man out of the village. They hunted all that day and were very successful.

This day established a pattern for the next few years. On the days that the man would hunt, the boy would follow. At first the boy would only watch. The man spoke very little. Even when the boy asked a question, the man seldom answered, so after a while the boy asked fewer and fewer questions. They just hunted together in silence, with the boy watching carefully.

But the man was an excellent teacher. He knew that the boy was very bright and very quick. Before long, the boy was imitating the man and contributing to the hunt.

The boy also watched the man in the village, especially the way he prepared and planned for the hunt. He watched the man carefully tend to his weapons and equipment. In a short time he was preparing his own equipment in the same way.

Within three years they were known as the best hunters in the village. They no longer hunted as leader and follower but as a team. Without speaking they knew what each would do in the hunt, and together they were more successful than either of them alone could be. Day by day, the man noted the growing confidence, skill, and strength of the boy. The man knew that the boy was destined to be a leader of the Valley People.

How will you teach the newcomers in your organization to "hunt"? One thing you can count on—they will be watching you closely. Whether you want it or not, they will learn their leadership and their self-leadership from you. Have you thought about what you want to teach them? Do you want to be a SuperLeader? Do you want them to be self-leaders and then SuperLeaders?

In this section, we begin our discussion about the implementation of SuperLeadership. That is, how does a SuperLeader actually carry out the ideas and concepts of leading others to lead themselves? We begin by trying to articulate the language of SuperLeadership. Most of all, we recognize that developing self-leadership is not an overnight process. It takes time and patience—and then more time and patience. We especially discuss the difficulties of transition from a more traditional top-down model to a SuperLeadership model.

THE LANGUAGE OF SUPERLEADERSHIP

Day in, day out, leaders interact with followers. Often we think of leadership as a particularly vivid moment in time, like Henry V addressing his troops or Martin Luther King, Jr., with his "I have a dream" speech. But for most of us, leadership is mainly expressed in the day-to-day verbal and nonverbal exchange between leader and follower.

In our research we have discovered certain patterns of behavior that characterize SuperLeadership. We know, for example, that a few thoughtless authoritarian remarks can destroy any relationship between an aspiring SuperLeader and followers. The most important pillar of SuperLeadership is the use of everyday conversation to enhance the confidence of followers and encourage them to undertake their own self-leadership practices. Here are a few tips about how everyday language and dialog can be used to enhance follower self-leadership:

- Reduce language that centers on direction, instruction, and command. Ask followers to provide their own direction: "What's next?" or "Where are you headed?"

- Listen more.

- Reduce the proportion of assigned goals. Ask a follower what his or her own goal is.

- In response to a failure or mistake, ask what can be learned. Use direct punitive language only as a last resort.

- Ask followers to orally work through their logic and analysis of how they have come to a decision. Be sure not to make this a quiz that provokes the follower's defensiveness.

- Ask followers to describe what other alternatives have been explored when they come to a decision.

- Ask about feelings: "How do you feel about that?"

- Overturn a follower's decision only as a last resort.

- Express confidence in a follower's potential and capacity to achieve a specific goal or accomplish a special task.

- Decline to directly solve a follower's problem unless it's a crisis, a last resort, or unless you alone have critical information. Ask followers to solve problems on their own or in collaboration with their peers.

- Decline to answer directly when asked by a follower to make a decision that should be made by the follower. Reflect the decision back onto the follower. Do express confidence in and support of followers and focus on opportunities for them to grow and learn. Don't let the follower put the "monkey" on your back.

▶ Ask followers if there are ways this job can be done more effectively.

▶ Verbally reinforce when a follower shows initiative. Look for opportunities to accept and implement follower initiative.

Sometimes people think that empowerment means permissiveness. Let's be clear and direct about this: We do not think of SuperLeadership as permissiveness, nor as *laissez faire*, but as an active involvement and interaction between leader and follower that concentrates on enhancing the follower's own self-leadership. The active involvement is expressed through the special language of the SuperLeader.

SuperLeadership and Mentoring

In some ways, SuperLeadership has similarities to the process of mentoring. Or perhaps it would be more accurate to say that mentoring is a form of SuperLeadership. The main purpose of traditional mentoring is for a more senior or experienced person to provide professional, career, and organizational advice to a younger or less experienced person. Most mentoring situations do not entail a dyad where the mentor is the direct supervisor of the junior person. Nevertheless, mentoring has typically focused on the development of the younger or less experienced person, which is also a purpose of SuperLeadership. In the information age, however, this pattern is shifting. Consider the following reverse-mentoring situation, where the traditional notions of leadership are turned upside down.

Recently, the *Wall Street Journal* reported an interesting program of reverse mentoring at the venerable organizational giant, General Electric.[1] Like other senior leaders drawn from an earlier generation, it's a challenge for GE's long-serving chairman Jack Welch, Jr., to enter the Internet age. Given his busy schedule, he had found it difficult to hone his Internet skills. His solution: get a mentor!

But as CEO, Welch was at the top of the GE pyramid. He couldn't look above for a mentor. So he reached out and asked Pam Wickham, a midlevel GE leader almost 20 years younger, for some personal instruction. After some hands-on tutoring from Wickham, Welch now brags about skills that many teenagers would find elementary: "I can do all kinds of sites, and I go to chat rooms and see what people are saying about GE."

In his usually zesty manner, Welch has attempted to convert other GE leaders to his newfound knowledge, and especially to his newly discovered mode of learning from below. He has "ordered" the top 600 leaders at GE to reach down in their ranks and find an Internet junkie to be their mentor.

There are some interesting lessons in this story that apply to the organizations of the 21st century. First, expertise is more and more unlikely to be represented by high position in an organizational hierarchy. In the old days, the boss was expected to know it all. Today, the most knowledgeable person may well be the individual lowest on the totem pole. The challenge lies in the question of how a hierarchy can release and make use of the knowledge possessed by every employee. In essence, every worker becomes a knowledge worker.

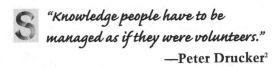

"*Knowledge people have to be managed as if they were volunteers.*"
—Peter Drucker[2]

Another lesson is that leadership is not the exclusive prerogative of those who are higher in a hierarchy. In the GE case, we can think of the more junior mentors as "leading" their elders, so it becomes a form of bottom-up leading. And in a later chapter on teams, we discuss lateral leading by peers as an important contemporary resource.

GUIDING THE TRANSITION TO SELF-LEADERSHIP

Developing self-leadership in others is not done overnight. The process is lengthy and complex, and requires patience and persistence. When a SuperLeader sets out to develop self-leadership in another, the transformation can be described as one with four stages:

1. Leader modeling of self-leadership behavior.

2. Guided participation of the follower by the leader.

3. Ensuring follower resources, training and capability.

4. Finally, follower self-leadership and performance.

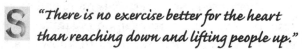

"There is no exercise better for the heart than reaching down and lifting people up."

—**John Andrew Holmes**[3]

Often, moving a follower toward self-leadership creates a dilemma for the leader. Inevitably, the time will come when the follower seems to be making a mistake; perhaps the follower sets an inappropriate goal, an incorrect target level, a questionable plan of action or undertakes a decision that is not well thought out. Recognizing the difficulty, the leader faces the choice of whether to intervene or to allow the follower to proceed. Of course the overall importance of the situation will have a bearing on the leader's final choice; the more critical the issue the more likely the leader is to intervene.

Here are some guidelines. To begin, the leader should ask a lot of questions. Generally, questions are less intimidating and power-oriented than outright rejection of the goal or plan of action, and they typically deliver an implicit message to the follower that something might be wrong without making a direct challenge. Questions help the follower to clarify consequences of projected courses of action or to detail specifics of the "action plan." Questions provide the follower with opportunities to reconsider previously chosen courses of action without undue threat.

But questions don't always evoke a change of direction and sometimes a follower remains committed to a course of action that, in the end, the leader believes is wrong. What next?

Generally, except under the most critical conditions, a Super-Leader will allow the follower to continue on her chosen course. We suggest that the leader's formal authority to change this course be used only when the decision has very serious consequences—that is, when it will cause damage, in the words of the very successful W.L. Gore and Associates, "below the waterline" (that threatens to sink the boat). In the long run, making mistakes is part of any learning process and it is an inevitable and necessary part of learning self-leadership. Hopefully, having made a mistake the follower will have gained a useful developmental experience and will be less likely to repeat the error.

An important factor is whether the type of culture exists where the follower can positively learn from mistakes. Organizations that encourage risk-taking are much more likely to find significant improvements in follower productivity and performance. Most of all, followers need to feel that making a mistake is not a "capital offense" but is only one (perhaps unpleasant) milestone leading toward the full maturity of their capability to be self-leaders.

During a follower's critical transition from traditional external leadership to self-leadership, previous dependency on superior authority needs to be unlearned. In its place, followers must develop a strong sense of confidence in their abilities to act on their own.

But frequently this transition is not very smooth, leaving the follower wondering why "the boss" is not providing more help and the leader biting his lip to avoid telling the follower to do the "right thing." Nevertheless, effective SuperLeaders sometimes *deliber-*

ately permit a course of action to proceed that at other times, in other places, they would not allow. To be self-leaders, followers must learn to stand on their own.

Once through this critical transition phase, the effects on the follower's performance can be remarkable. Followers develop a much better understanding of the full range of their own capabilities and of the demands of their surroundings. Most of all, exercising their own self-leadership produces a motivation and psychological commitment that energizes followers to greater and greater achievements. SuperLeaders who have successfully unleashed the power of self-led followers understand the ultimate reward and satisfaction of managing these individuals. Furthermore, they can see beyond the problem of living with the difficult days of transition into self-leadership.

In the long run, making mistakes is part of any learning process and it is an inevitable and necessary part of learning self-leadership.

The process of change in becoming a SuperLeader is not easy. Consider the following true account of a corporate leader vice president, who described how he felt and what happened to him as he underwent this change on the road to SuperLeadership.[4]

One of the first steps is to recognize one's over-involvement, compulsiveness, and unwillingness to let go: "I'm involved in a great many projects in my company and I can't do them casually."

It's important to be candid about one's own motivation. "Thinking about this compulsion, I realized I don't do it for the money, nor do I have ambition any longer for promotion. It's something in me ..." he explained. "I am sure that at least part of my problem is that I am still seeking 'stroking' . . . approval. . . . I'm still anxious that my bosses know when I do something well. I get especially upset if someone gets credit for something that I believe I did."

He reflects further, beginning to sound like a SuperLeader: "I think there is a way I call it making myself into a 'backroom person'. . . . Now I'm attempting to become a person who makes things happen without appearing to be there. . . . I work hard at making myself invisible.

"When someone says, 'Gee, we sure have been lucky getting this done' and I know it got done because of my behind-the-scenes phone calls, meetings, and reports, I am beginning to experience pleasure," he continued. "When I con-centrate on my new role as *éminence grise*, my yearning to say 'Hey I did it' diminishes. This allows me to make contributions with less stress."

A mature SuperLeader becomes more indirect. "My way of dealing with it is to think of myself as a combination coach/spectator. What that means is that I spend a lot of time listening before I do anything. When someone describes a plan of action that I think is incorrect, I don't take the plan apart and substitute my own. I let the speaker finish and wait to hear what the others have to say. Usually, if I see something wrong, someone else will too."

"I recognize that this approach has its risks. I may hide myself so successfully that people will start to wonder what I'm doing and decide I'm not necessary. It is also possible that the effort to be silent and to relinquish credit may take more out of me than an excess of activity. So far though, that has not been the case. . . . [I've] learned a great deal. . . . I gathered information that I don't think I could have gotten any other way. I was more involved in what was [really] going on. . . . I was in an improved situation relative to the business."

MacGregor—Insisting On Self-Leadership

Elliott Carlisle

This classic profile was included in our original version of SuperLeadership *and was, in many ways, ahead of its time. MacGregor provides a striking example of leadership that not only promotes and expects self-leadership from followers but insists on it.*

My encounter with MacGregor came about during the course of a study of the extent to which operating managers actually use participative management techniques in their dealings with subordinates.

MacGregor, who at the time was manager of one of the largest refineries in the country, was the last of more than 100 managers I interviewed in the course of the study.

The switchboard operator answered with the name of the refinery. When I asked for MacGregor's office, a male voice almost instantly said "Hello." I then asked for MacGregor, whereupon the voice responded, "This is he." I should have recognized at once that this was no ordinary manager; he answered his own phone instantly, as though he had been waiting for it to ring. To my question about when it would be convenient for me to come see him, he replied, 'Any time.' I said, "Would today be all right?" His response was, "Today, tomorrow, or Wednesday would be OK; or you could come Thursday, except don't come between 10:00 A.M. and noon; or you could come Friday or next week any time."

I took MacGregor at his word and drove over immediately to see him without any further announcement of my visit. As I entered his office, he turned slowly and said, "You must be Carlisle. The head office told me you wanted to talk to me about the way we run things here. Sit down and fire away."

MACGREGOR'S MODUS OPERANDI

"Do you hold regular meetings with your subordinates?" I asked.

"Yes, I do," he replied.

"How often?" I asked.

"Once a week, on Thursdays, between 10:00 A.M. and noon; that's why I couldn't see you then," was his response.

"What sorts of things do you discuss?" I queried, following my interview guide.

"My subordinates tell me about the decisions they've made during the past week," he explained.

"Then you believe in participative decision making," I commented.

"No, as a matter of fact, I don't," said MacGregor.

"Then why hold the meetings?" I asked. "Why not just tell your people about the operating decisions you've made and let them know how to carry them out?"

"Oh, I don't make their decisions for them and I just don't believe in participating in the decisions they should be making, either; we hold the weekly meeting so that I can keep informed on what they're doing and how. The meeting also gives me a chance to appraise their technical and managerial abilities," he explained.

> S *"I used to make all the operating decisions myself, but I quit doing that a few years ago when I discovered that I didn't have enough time to do my own job."*

"Now that I've quit making other people's decisions, I can concentrate on my own work."

"You don't make operating decisions anymore?" I asked in astonishment.

"No," he replied. Sensing my incredulity, he added, "Obviously you don't believe me. Why not ask one of my subordinates? Which one do you want to talk to?"

"I haven't any idea; I don't even know how many subordinates you have, let alone their names. You choose one," I suggested.

"No, I wouldn't do that—for two reasons. First, I don't make decisions. And second, when my subordinate confirms that I don't make decisions, you'll say that it's a put-up job. So here is a list of my eight immediate subordinates, the people who report directly to me. Choose one name from it and I'll call him and you can talk to him," said MacGregor.

"OK—Johnson, then. I'll talk to him if he's free," said I.

"I'm sure he's able to talk to you. I'll call him and tell him you're on the way over." Reaching for the phone, he determined that Johnson would be happy to have someone to talk to.

EMPLOYEE VIEWS OF MACGREGOR

I walked over to Johnson's unit and found him to be in his early thirties. After a few minutes of casual conversation, I discovered that MacGregor and all eight of his subordinates were chemical engineers. Johnson said, "I suppose MacGregor gave you that bit about his not making decisions, didn't he? That man is a gas."

"It isn't true though, is it? He does make decisions, doesn't he?" I asked.

"No, he doesn't; everything he told you is true. He simply decided not to get involved in decisions that his subordinates are being paid to make. So he stopped making them," said Johnson.

Then I asked Johnson whether he tried to get MacGregor to make a decision and his response was:

"Only once. I had been on the job for only about a week when I ran into an operating problem I couldn't solve, so I phoned MacGregor. He answered the phone with that sleepy 'Hello' of his. I told him who I was and that I had a problem. His response was instantaneous: 'Good, that's what you're being paid to do: solve problems,' and then he hung up. I was dumbfounded. I didn't really know any of the people I was working with, so because I didn't think I had any other alternative I called him back, got the same sleepy 'Hello,' and again identified myself. He replied sharply, 'I thought I told you that you were paid to solve problems.'"

 "Do you think that I should do your job as well as my own?"

"When I insisted on seeing him about my problem, he answered, 'I don't know how you expect me to help you. You have a technical problem and I don't make operating decisions about the refinery anymore. Ask one of the other men. They're all in touch with what goes on out there.'

"I didn't know which one to consult, so I insisted again on seeing him. He finally agreed—grudgingly—to see me right away, so I went over to his office and there he was in his characteristic looking-out-the-window posture. When I sat down he saw that I was determined to involve him in my problems, so he sat down on the sofa in front of his coffee table and, pen in hand, prepared to write on a pad of paper. He asked me to state precisely what the problem was and he wrote down exactly what I said. Then he asked what the conditions for its solution were. I replied that I didn't know what he meant by that question. His response was, 'If you don't know what conditions have to be satisfied for a solution to be reached, how do you know when you've solved the problem?' I told him I'd never thought of approaching a problem that way and he replied, 'Then you'd better start. I'll work through this one with you this time, but don't expect me to do your problem solving for you because that's your job, not mine.'

"I stumbled through the conditions that would have to be satisfied by the solution. Then he asked me what alternative approaches I could think of. I gave him the first one I could think of—let's call it X—and he wrote it down and asked me what would happen if I did X. I replied with my answer—let's call it A. Then he asked me how A compared with the conditions I had established for the solution of the problem. I replied that it did not meet them. MacGregor told me that I'd have to think of another. I came up with Y, which I said would yield result B, and this still fell short of the solution conditions. After more prodding from MacGregor, I came up with Z, which I said would have C as a result; although this clearly came a lot closer to the conditions I had established for the solution than any of the others I'd suggested, it still did not satisfy all of them. MacGregor then asked me if I could combine any of the approaches I'd suggested. I replied I could do X and Z and then saw that the resultant A plus C would indeed satisfy all the solution conditions I had set up previously. When I thanked MacGregor, he replied, 'What for? Get the hell out of my office; you could have done that bit of problem solving perfectly well without wasting my time. Next time you really can't solve a problem on your own, ask the Thursday man and then tell me about it at the Thursday meeting.'"

I asked Johnson about Mr. MacGregor's reference to the Thursday man.

"That's the person who runs the Thursday meeting when MacGregor is away from the plant. I'm the Thursday man now. My predecessor left here about two months ago."

"Where did he go? Did he quit the company?" I asked.

"God, no. He got a refinery of his own. That's what happens to a lot of Thursday men. After the kind of experience we get coping with everyone's problems, and MacGregor's refusal to do what he perceives as his subordinates' work, we don't need an operating superior anymore, and we're ready for our own refineries. Incidentally, most of the people at our level have adopted MacGregor's method in dealing with our own direct reports."

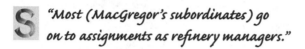

"Most (MacGregor's subordinates) go on to assignments as refinery managers."

I went back to see MacGregor. He turned and asked, "Well, now do you believe that I don't make any decisions?"

I said, "No, that could have been just a fluke." He suggested I see another subordinate, and asked me to pick another name from the list. I picked Peterson who, when phoned, said she was available, so I went to her office.

Peterson was in her late twenties. She asked me what I thought of MacGregor. I said I found him most unusual. Peterson replied, "Yes, he's a gas." Peterson's story paralleled Johnson's; that is, MacGregor refused to make decisions related to the work of his subordinates. When Peterson got into a situation she could not deal with, she said she called one of the other supervisors, usually Johnson, and together they worked it out. At the Thursday meetings she reported on the decision and gave credit to her helper. "If I hadn't," she added, "I probably wouldn't get help from that quarter again."

In reply to a query on what the Thursday meetings were like, she said, "Well, we all sit around that big conference table in MacGregor's office. He sits at the head like a thinned-down Buddha, and we go around the table talking about the decisions we've made and, if we got help, who helped us. The other guys occasionally make comments, especially if the particular decision being discussed was like one they had had to make themselves at some point or if it had some direct effect on their own operations." MacGregor had said very little at these past few meetings, according to Peterson, but he did pass on any new developments that he heard about at the head office.

HEAD-OFFICE ASSESSMENT OF MACGREGOR

By the time I had finished with Johnson and Peterson, it was time for lunch. I decided I'd go downtown and stop in at the head office to try to find out their assessment of MacGregor and his operation. I visited the operations chief for the corporation. I had wanted to thank him for his willingness to go along with my study, anyway. When I told him I had met MacGregor, his immediate response was, "Isn't he a gas?" I muttered something about having heard that comment before and asked him about the efficiency of MacGregor's operation in comparison with that of other refineries in the corporation. His response was instantaneous. "Oh, MacGregor has by far the most efficient producing unit."

"Is that because he has the newest equipment?" I asked.

"No. As a matter of fact he has the oldest in the corporation. His was the first refinery we built."

MORE POINTERS ON MACGREGOR'S STYLE OF MANAGING

I went back to the refinery with a few last questions for MacGregor.

"Now let me focus a bit more on your role as refinery manager. You say you don't make decisions. Suppose a subordinate told you at a Thursday meeting about a decision he'd made and you were convinced that it was a mistake. What would you do about it?"

"How much would the mistake cost me?"

"Oh, I don't know," I answered.

"Can't tell you, then. It would depend on how much it would cost."

"Say, $3,000," I suggested.

"That's easy, I'd let him make it," said MacGregor. I sensed I'd hit the upper limit before MacGregor either would have moved in himself or, more likely, would have suggested that the subordinate discuss it with the Thursday man and then report back to him on their joint decision.

"When was the last time you let a subordinate make a mistake of that magnitude?" I asked skeptically.

"About four weeks ago," said MacGregor.

"You let someone who works for you make such a serious mistake? Why did you do that?"

"Three reasons," said MacGregor. "First, I was only 99.44 percent sure it would be a mistake and if it hadn't turned out to be one, I'd have felt pretty foolish. Second, I thought that making a mistake like this one would be such a tremendous learning experience for him that he'd never make another like that one again. I felt it would do him more good than signing him up for most of the management development courses that are available. Third, this is a profit center. It was early in the budget year and I felt that we could afford it."

"What was the result?" I asked.

"It was a mistake—and I heard about it in short order from the controller downtown by phone." (I realized suddenly that during the whole time I had been in the office, neither MacGregor's phone nor his secretary's had rung.)

"The controller said, 'MacGregor how could you let a stupid mistake like that last one slip through?'"

"What did you say?"

"Well, I figured a good attack is the best defense." I asked him which refinery in the corporation was the most efficient. He replied, "You know yours is. That has nothing to do with it." I told him that it had everything to do with it.

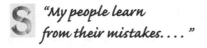

S *"My people learn from their mistakes. . . . "*

"Until the rest of the plants in the organization started operating at the same degree of efficiency as this one, I wasn't going to waste my time talking to clerks. Then I hung up."

"What happened?"

"Well, relations were a bit strained for a while—but they know I'm probably the best refinery manager in the business and I can get another job anytime, so it blew over pretty quickly," he said, not without a degree of self-satisfaction.

MACGREGOR'S CONTROL SYSTEMS

"Peterson told me you have quite a control system here. How does it work?" I asked.

"Very simply," said MacGregor. "On Wednesdays at 2:00 P.M. my subordinates and I get the printout from the computer, which shows the production men their output against quota and the maintenance superintendent his costs to date against the budget. If there is an unfavorable gap between the two, they call me about 3:00 P.M. and the conversation goes something like this: 'Mr. MacGregor, I know I have a problem and this is what I'm going to do about it.' If their solution will work, I tell them to go ahead. If not, I tell them so and then they go and work on it some more and then call back. If the new one will work, I tell them to go ahead with it. If not, I suggest they get in touch with one of the other men, work it out together, and then call me and tell me how they are going to deal with it. If that doesn't work, I refer them to the Thursday man. That way I don't get involved in making operating decisions.

"I used to have a smaller refinery than this one, where I found myself frantically busy all the time—answering the phone constantly and continually doing my subordinates' problem-solving for them. They were always more than willing to let me do their work because it was easier than doing it themselves, and also because if the solution did not work out then I was to blame. Can't fault them for trying that. But when I came here, I resolved to get myself out of that kind of rat race and set about designing this system. I worked out a computer-based production control system in conjunction with a set of quotas I negotiate each year with each of my operating people, and a cost budget with the maintenance man. Then I arranged for Wednesday reports. Sometimes it takes a bit of time to renegotiate these quotas—and I've been known to use peer pressure to get them to a reasonable level—but these performance objectives really have to be accepted by the individual before they have any legitimacy or motivational value for him.

"I can't even remember when I've had to get directly involved myself with their work. I do a lot of reading related to my work. That's why, when they call me with solutions, I can usually tell accurately whether or not their proposals are going to work out. A lot of managers feel that they have to keep proving to their people that they know more about their subordinates' jobs than the subordinates themselves by doing their work for them. I refuse to do that anymore."

MacGregor illustrates SuperLeadership in several interesting ways. Most of all, he is committed to a leadership philosophy that depends for its success on developing effective subordinates. His employees demonstrate an unusual ability to work on their own in a highly effective and responsible manner.

MacGregor doesn't just encourage his subordinates to work independently—to be self-leaders—he absolutely insists on it.

More specifically, MacGregor relies on his own tailor-made versions of many of the strategies we have presented in this book. To begin with, he is an excellent model for his subordinates. He demonstrates through his own behavior a commitment to self-leadership and to solving his own problems. Further, his dramatically unique style of leading others is being adopted in turn by his managers in dealing with their own subordinates. His approach centers on fostering subordinate growth and independence by facilitating their full abilities to solve their own problems and to make their own decisions. One clear measure of MacGregor's long-term success is that his subordinates often go on to be highly effective managers of their own refineries.

MacGregor also reinforces his subordinates for their independent efforts. In particular, he makes it a practice to recognize and give credit to his employees for their self-led accomplishments in their weekly Thursday meetings. Further, he is very committed to goal setting. Indeed, his control system largely centers around helping his employees to establish their own challenging performance objectives and providing concrete feedback on their progress. Again, however, he insists that his subordinates reach these goals by means of their own decisions and efforts. MacGregor views mistakes, even relatively costly ones, as an investment in his subordinates' learning and growth.

Finally, MacGregor has clearly facilitated the development of a high-performance culture based on self-leadership. Employees recognize taking personal responsibility, working independently, and exercising self-control as strongly entrenched cultural norms. Over time, self-leadership became the normal way of doing things. His refinery has become a model for others in the company and his leadership a model for aspiring SuperLeaders.

8 Leading Individuals to Become Self-Leaders

HOW DID **GENERAL DWIGHT D. EISENHOWER** become such an admired leader? In the years prior to World War II, we can trace the development of Eisenhower's leadership style. As he absorbed the military environment he learned to be delegated to and, in turn, to delegate authority. Ike learned leadership through exposure to models that strongly facilitated his own self-leadership skills.[1]

One of the greatest influences and most important models in Eisenhower's life and career was General George C. Marshall. Their relationship has been described variously as being like that of father and son, leader and protégé, and partners. Undoubtedly, Eisenhower learned much from Marshall.

From the very start, Marshall let it be known that he wanted no yes-men in his camp. On Eisenhower's first day at the War Plans Department at the beginning of World War II, Marshall called him into his office and asked Ike what the United States' Philippine strategy should be. Eisenhower spent the day at his desk, then returned with an analysis of the Philippine situation and a recommended strategy. Marshall was pleased with Ike's response to the task: "Eisenhower, the Department is filled with able men who analyze their problems well but feel compelled always to bring them to me for final solution. I must have assistants who will solve their own problems and tell me later what they have done."[2] Ike understood the significance of autonomy, of "owning" a job and doing it well in his own style.

As he had done under other commanders, Eisenhower completed his own tasks with a minimum of supervision. When his time came to command, he expected the same from his subordinates. "What General Marshall wanted most ... were senior officers who would take the responsibility for action in their own areas of competence without coming to him for the final decision; officers who in their turn would have enough sense to delegate the details of their decisions to their subordinates."[3]

Learning to lead from those above him, Ike carried this sense of delegation and control over into his own leadership style.

It is clear that General Eisenhower learned much of his leadership from his mentor, General George C. Marshall. How did you learn your own leadership? More importantly, are you aware of how your leadership is influencing others, especially those who are younger and less experienced than you?

Most of all, the SuperLeader is concerned with unleashing the power of self-leadership in others. Even if we understand the philosophy and concept of SuperLeadership intellectually, in the end it's action that counts. What do SuperLeaders actually *do* in order to develop follower self-leadership?

This is the first of three chapters that attempts to answer that question. In the following chapter, we concentrate on teams as vehicles for self-leadership. We address the issue of team leadership and discuss structural changes like self-managed teams, virtual teams, and cross-functional teams, all of which have been important historical vehicles for enhancing self-leadership. Then, in a separate chapter we focus on the organization as a whole, and especially deal with the issue of how an organizational culture can be instrumental in enhancing or retarding self-leadership.

In this chapter we concentrate mainly on a dyadic model of leadership—that is, a leader and an individual follower. We ask the question of *how* to cultivate self-leadership in others. To answer this question we turn to ideas about behavioral modeling, goal setting, rewards, and thought patterns.

DEVELOPING SELF-LEADERSHIP THROUGH MODELING

How do leaders learn to lead? Most of us can and do learn from reading or classroom-oriented instruction. But for leaders in organizations, leadership is mainly learned through observing others. This is a fundamental learning process that we first encounter as children when we observe and learn from our parents. Leaders have a special responsibility to pass on the appropriate "lore" and culture of organizational leadership. As in ancient tribes, this knowledge is mainly transmitted through modeling. Modeling is a process where a behavior is learned by observing another perform the behavior.

Typically, learning through modeling is unsystematic and haphazard. It occurs without conscious direction and effort. Nevertheless, because of its pervasiveness and power, it can be very useful if leaders understand the modeling process and use it in a deliberate manner. The opening story of this chapter about Dwight D. Eisenhower is about how he learned his special form of leadership from his mentor, General George C. Marshall.

The fundamental characteristic of modeling is that learning takes place not by actually experiencing self-leadership but by observing the self-leadership of another, especially a person with high status or position. Over time, followers associate the behavior they actually see with "correct" leadership and success in the company. Thus, a primary force in learning self-leadership is the self-leadership actually modeled by a leader.

Sometimes, a particularly prominent leader attracts special attention and even "cult" status. Consider the following headline and story about how fledgling CEOs want to imitate Bill Gates, even to the point where they copy the "warts" as well as the "winning ways."[4]

The headline shouted, "Bill Gates' Executive Style Inspires a Cult Following." The story that followed detailed how CEOs of aspiring start-up companies wanted to capture the charisma of the Gates mystique for themselves and their companies.

One of these CEOs is Naveen Jain, former Microsoft executive who now runs his own Internet services company, InfoSpace, Inc. Jain has concluded that a high-tech executive should have the charisma of a cult leader. According to the article, the Gates leadership style has been mimicked by Jain and hundreds of technology start-ups.

"It's as if you took a DNA sample from the chief executive and blew it up to monstrous size," says Marc Andreessen, another former Microsoft executive who now heads his own company. "The founder and the company share all the same strengths and weaknesses."

The imitation follows critical as well as admirable qualities. For example, in the InfoSpace lobby a wall hanging features a magazine story about Jain that includes the following Jain quote: "I think most people think of me as an arrogant [expletive], and that's the perception I want. It says don't mess with me or you'll be crushed." Clearly Jain has taken the measure of Gates, his model.

 Learning takes place not by actually experiencing the target behavior, but by observing . . . another's behavior.

Generally, modeling can be considered a positive or constructive form of learning. Robert Waterman, author of many management books, recognized this:

As humans, we seem to learn in two ways: First, by analyzing our shortcomings and trying to correct them and second, by observing those who do things best and trying to imitate them.

Recalling dimly my days as a ski instructor, I would look at it like this: When I took my class on the hill and said, "You're falling down too much and here's why," they would learn something. But they would learn only half the lesson. They'd learn the rest when I showed them what it looks like when it's done right. It's that second half that we are searching for in management.[5]

Modeling is an essential part of SuperLeadership. Leaders can make deliberate and productive use of modeling in their quest to develop the self-leadership of followers.

In the development of follower self-leadership, modeling can be used on a day-to-day basis in several ways. The first use is in establishing new behaviors, especially self-leadership behaviors, in followers. The second involves strengthening the likelihood that followers will continue to use positive behaviors they have already learned. This is facilitated when the follower observes positive results and rewards received by a model for performing desired behaviors. But in addition, modeling can be used in a more formal, deliberate manner through training.

Unfortunately, modeling can also create negative results if it is not well understood and managed. Consider the following case, which is based on real events that occurred in a U.S. department-store company. It's a story of imitation of negative leader behavior.

━━━━━━━━

Tom, the new systems analyst, was uncomfortable and confused about the occasional punitive management style of Jim, the group leader. Jim's behavior seemed inconsistent with his otherwise friendly and pleasant personality. Tom began to understand the situation only after witnessing several incidents over a few weeks.

One day when Jim was out visiting a client, a newspaper ad ran with the wrong information for his department. Tom was called into the division manager's office the first thing that morning. "Where's Jim?" the division manager demanded. "He's on a client trip," Tom responded nervously.

"Well, you tell him to get his fanny in here as soon as he gets back!"

"Uh, OK," Tom said timidly.

"What the hell do you think you guys are doing anyhow, giving advertising the wrong information?"

The chewing-out continued for about five minutes. What struck Tom was that the division manager didn't really seem that mad; he just appeared to be acting like he was. He seemed to be intentionally raking Tom over the coals as a conscious leadership strategy.

A few weeks later, a division meeting was held with the group vice president to go over department plans that would be presented to the president in a couple of days. The vice president was very critical, especially of Jim. When Jim finished presenting his material, he was informed that the president would "tear him apart." Interestingly, when the presentation was actually made, the president found another target—the same vice president who had been so critical of Jim.

"Didn't you tell them to address the impact of our new strategic plan on their departments?" he snapped. "How in the hell do you expect us to make a profit if you don't manage your people?"

At this point the picture was becoming much clearer for Tom. Having now seen the entire chain of punitive command in action, he could understand Jim's leadership behavior a little better. A punitive leadership style was being passed down by example, from level to level and from one management generation to the next.

The final blow came one day after lunch when Tom was standing in front of a company bulletin board with a couple of friends he had been trained with.

"Look at this. Smith was promoted to divisional leader in hard goods," one of the friends commented. "I think that was a real mistake," he continued. "I don't think he can be tough enough and get on his people the way he'll have to, to get the work out in that division. He's just too nice of a guy."

Tom stared at his friend uncomfortably. "This guy wouldn't have thought that way a few months ago," Tom thought. "He was really friendly and supportive when he first came, but he's changed." It seemed clear that a punitive leadership philosophy was being modeled and learned throughout the entire company. In that moment the whole organization looked different. Tom left the company a short time later.

Leaders have a special responsibility to pass on the appropriate "culture." This knowledge is mainly transmitted through modeling.

Thinking about modeling gives us valuable insights about how we can fulfill the SuperLeader role. The primary objective is to provide an effective self-leadership example for others, for the purpose of facilitating the development of their self-leadership capabilities. The checklist summary below provides a guide of how we can use modeling in our SuperLeadership role.

- Capture the attention of others. Establish yourself as a credible self-leadership model: if you want others to be effective self-leaders, be a credible example of self-leadership yourself. Display self-leadership behaviors in a vivid, detailed, and understandable manner.

- Facilitate the retention of modeled self-leadership behaviors. Encourage others to physically and mentally rehearse self-leadership behavior.

- Facilitate practical applications of self-leadership. Provide opportunities and encourage others to use self-leadership behavior when appropriate.

- Provide motivation for putting self-leadership into practice. Facilitate the availability of external, vicarious, and self-generated incentives.

DEVELOPING SELF-LEADERSHIP THROUGH GOAL SETTING

Goal setting is a critical part of SuperLeadership. Research and experience show that setting specific goals generally leads to higher performance than if no goals or ambiguous goals are used. Moderately difficult goals generally lead to higher performance than easy or impossible goals. And, participation in goal setting is thought to enhance follower willingness to attain the goal. David Packard, the late cofounder of Hewlett-Packard, describes how his company used interactive goal setting during its early days: "These objectives were not things that [were] dictated, these were ideas that we generated working together with people. . . . I believe it's very important, that if people have some part in making the decisions that they're going to be involved with they're going to be much more effective in implementing those decisions."[6]

A major challenge for a SuperLeader is to develop the capability of followers to realistically set their own goals, including goals for their own self-leadership development. The transition from assigned goals to self-set goals can be very difficult, but followers need to have some latitude in making mistakes during this critical period. Sometimes a SuperLeader may even deliberately withhold goals from followers as a planned strategy to develop their self-leadership. Perhaps the most critical factor of all is whether the SuperLeader sets a personal goal to encourage and facilitate a follower's own goal setting.

An important point to note is that goal setting is something to be *learned*; that is, a skill that followers can develop over a period of time. Goal setting is not necessarily an innate behavior that every new employee brings to the job. Since goal setting is something to be learned, the role of the SuperLeader is to serve as a model, coach, and teacher.

S *"Did you ever hear of a man who had striven all his life . . . toward an object, and in no measure obtained it? If a man constantly aspires, is he not elevated?"*

—Henry David Thoreau[7]

Teaching followers how to set goals can follow the general framework that we have established earlier: first, followers are provided with a model to emulate; second, they are allowed guided participation; and finally, they assume the targeted self-leadership skill, which in this case is setting their own goal.

Note that we begin with modeling, which as we previously discussed is a key element in learning new skills. Because of their formal position of authority, SuperLeaders have a special responsibility to personally demonstrate their own goal-setting behavior in a way that can be emulated by other employees. It's unrealistic to expect an employee to use goals when the leader is not using them. Furthermore, goals need to be coordinated among the different levels of the hierarchy. Follower goals, even those that are self-set, need to be consistent with higher-level and organizational goals.

Goal setting by employees is a recurring theme in the general employee-participation literature. It is a fundamental part of the philosophy that employees can be more motivated and achieve higher performance if they participate in decisions that subsequently affect their lives at work. But the major point here is that a SuperLeader can play a key role in helping followers to learn to set their own goals.

DEVELOPING SELF-LEADERSHIP THROUGH REWARDS

Eric Raymond, accomplished hacker and provocative writer, has reflected on how programmers can be motivated. He especially considers the limitations of Transactor type leadership. "You cannot motivate the best people with money. Money is just a way to keep score." He is especially convinced of the motivating potential that comes from natural rewards: "People enjoy tasks, especially creative tasks, when the tasks are in the optimal-challenge zone: not too hard, not too easy. . . . People do their best work when they are passionately engaged in what they are doing."[8]

For the most part, conventional viewpoints about using organizational rewards tend to focus on target behaviors that are very task related; that is, we want to reward people for good performance. One prominent example is incentive pay systems. Incentives are only one example of an array of rewards that organizations use to reward employees (see table on next page).

We are basically in sympathy with the idea that material rewards should be used to reward job-related target behaviors. However, rewards take on a more sophisticated perspective when seen

Organizational Rewards

Material	Fringe Benefits	Status Symbols	Social/ Interpersonal	Natural Rewards (e.g., from the task)	Self- Administered
Pay	Medical plan	Corner office	Informal recognition	Sense of competence, self-control, and purpose resulting from a pleasant work environment and interesting, challenging tasks	Self-recognition
Pay raise	Company automobile insurance	Office with window	Praise		Self-praise
Stock options	Pension contributions	Carpeting	Smiles		Self-congratulations
Profit sharing	Product discount plans	Drapes	Evaluative feedback		Self-administered physical rewards (e.g., a break, a cup of coffee . . .)
Bonus plans	Vacation trips	Paintings	Compliments	Job with more responsibility	
Incentive plans	Recreation facilities	Watches	Nonverbal signals	Job rotation	Self-administered cognitive rewards (e.g., imagining favorite vacation spot, imagining receiving recognition at an award ceremony . . .)
Christmas bonus	Work breaks	Rings	Pat on the back	Output feedback	
	Club privileges		Ask for suggestions		
	Expenses		Invitations to coffee/lunch		
			Newspaper article		
			Formal awards/ recognition		
			Wall plaque		

through the eyes of the SuperLeader. If the purpose of the Super-Leader is to lead others to self-leadership, then an essential ingredient of SuperLeadership is to teach followers how to reward themselves and to build natural rewards into their work. This philosophy is much less obsessed with relying on external reward systems to influence followers.

The characteristics of SuperLeader reward systems are thus somewhat different from those of more traditional reward systems. The SuperLeader attempts to emphasize self-administered and natural rewards and, in a comparative sense, de-emphasize externally administered rewards. Thus the focus of the reward system shifts from the left side of the chart to the right side, from material and fringe types of rewards to a stronger emphasis on natural rewards that stem more from the task itself, and from self-administration of rewards.

There is a different type of dependency relationship between leaders and followers within a traditional hierarchy: even a high-performing follower is relatively dependent upon the power, authority, information, and ability of the leader. High performance is maintained through a leadership system that focuses on unambiguous directions and goals from the leader, with rewards based on performance clearly controlled by the leader. In Chapter 2 we referred to this approach as Transactor leadership. Overall, research has shown that this approach can produce high-performing followers. Nevertheless, it is a system of hierarchical dependency that, consistent with bureaucracies, tends to produce task-focused conformists and frequently minimizes creativity and innovation. Followers become very good at following orders under a traditional leader who emphasizes short-term task performance at the expense of long-term effectiveness.

S *An essential ingredient of SuperLeadership is to teach followers how to reward themselves.*

The SuperLeader, on the other hand, develops an entirely different relationship with followers based on interdependence rather than dependence. Within an overall system of goals and rewards, followers who have developed their self-leadership skills are much more focused on self-set goals, self-design of tasks, and self-administered rewards. These self-directed individuals are quite different from the high-performing conformists of the traditional leadership situation. While self-leading employees can be distressing to more traditional leaders because they may seem less controllable, Super-Leaders will tend to appreciate them for their creativity, innovation, and productivity as they strive to unleash and maximize their self-leadership.

The way rewards are used can also play an important role in the development of self-leadership capabilities in others. First, direct reward of self-leadership is necessary and appropriate. Second, rewards can also be used to establish and highlight models to send a message about what behavior is desirable. Consider the following example, which is based on an incident we actually observed at a computer manufacturing facility:

I sensed that the weekly team meeting was nearing its end. Mary, the team leader, had conducted the meeting, which mainly consisted of informal reports from various members of the 23-person team. The commitment of the team members to improvement was obvious.

But the most interesting aspect of the meeting was the evident pride of several production workers as they stood and made their reports. Obviously not experienced public speakers, they were somewhat uncomfortable with this new role. Nevertheless they stood, "spoke their piece," and were very pleased to have conquered this small but important personal challenge. Each speaker was reinforced by the nonverbal behavior of those sitting nearby.

Mary turned the meeting over to Fred, the assistant team leader. As Fred stood, the broad smile on his face and his special manner hinted at a pleasant surprise. Curiosity and attention in the room picked up. "As you know," said Fred, "our company has a quarterly 'Outstanding Performer' club. Last quarter there were 35 winners, and you may remember that the winners (with friends and spouses) attended Mardi Gras in New Orleans. This quarter, the winners will be taking a four-day, escorted group trip to the Calgary Stampede.

"I'm very pleased to announce today that our plant has its first member of the Outstanding Performers Club." The anticipation in the room was electric. "Of course, this award is for all-around performance but in this case, special consideration was given because the candidate, on her own, developed the special pretesting procedure for the xxx subassembly. This short pre-test reduced the reject rate on this subassembly from 35 percent to less than two percent." Fred ceremoniously tore open the large envelope he was holding. "Mrs. Louise Newman, would you please come up and accept your certificate and your tickets to the Calgary Stampede!"

I was amazed at the intensity of the spontaneous applause as a small, grandmotherly, gray-haired lady rose to accept the award. Afterward she was surrounded by other team members, whose kisses and congratulations were natural and sincere. It occurred to me that the Academy Awards must be like this!

This incident exemplifies publicly rewarding self-leadership behavior. In Louise's case, the specific behavior was the development of a pre-testing procedure. She had developed this procedure using her own initiative—she acted as a self-leader.

There were several rewards in this incident; first, of course, the paid vacation trip to the Calgary Stampede. In addition, the certificate is a symbolic reward. But perhaps the most important reward of all was the public recognition that Louise received from the organization and her peers. Another important point is that Fred went out of his way to link the rewards to specific self-leadership behaviors, in this case the self-initiated development of the pretesting procedure.

Rewards can be used to send a message to others that self-leadership is appropriate.

The lesson from this story is straightforward. Followers learn from and are motivated by rewards they observe given to others for the performance of self-leadership behaviors. Indeed, leaders can learn to use this principle by remembering the often-quoted "praise in public" approach. Public praise can be a powerful motivating force for others to initiate self-leadership actions.

DEVELOPING SELF-LEADERSHIP THROUGH POSITIVE THOUGHT PATTERNS

Constructive thought patterns are an essential component of self-leadership. Sometimes, especially at the early stages of employment, employees do not naturally think constructively about themselves. They have doubts and fears and a general lack of confidence in themselves. At this stage, the actions of the SuperLeader are critical: his or her positive comments sometimes must serve as a temporary surrogate for the follower's own constructive thought patterns.

The SuperLeader creates productive thought patterns by carefully expressing confidence in the follower's ability, which can act to extend her present level of competence. Support and encouragement are necessary. In many ways, this expression of confidence is the essence of the guided-participation phase of teaching each follower to lead herself.

Here's another case where a sensitive leader helps a follower to use productive patterns of thought, this time to overcome his anxiety about speaking before a group—a fear shared, according to some estimates, by perhaps as many as 85 percent of all people.

"Oh, Helen," exclaimed Keith, "I'm never going to be able to do it." Keith and Helen were talking about Keith's assignment to make his first presentation to the Finance Committee. Since Keith worked for Helen, she was particularly concerned that he do well—both for Keith's sake and for the reputation of her department. She knew that the development of Keith's presentation skills was an important ingredient in Keith's career advancement.

"Public speaking used to bother me, too," replied Helen. "I thought I would die when I was assigned my first briefing."

Keith was skeptical because he knew that Helen was a highly regarded presenter. "I don't believe it," he said. "Everybody knows how good you are."

"I'm not kidding," said Helen. "I was shaking in my boots during my first presentation, but I managed to stumble through. I knew I needed to get help, so I asked for some help from a senior manager who I knew was good at presentations. He gave me some instruction, and I learned a lot."

"Like what?" asked Keith.

"Well, I learned some physical things, like using keyword notes and not memorizing or reading. I learned how to use visual aids like PowerPoint slides. I made eye contact with the audience. I found that using a pointer helped relieve my anxiety about what to do with my hands. But the part that really helped me the most was the way I changed my thinking about making a speech."

"Changed your thinking!" exclaimed Keith. "What do you mean by that?"

"First, I tried to think of my presentation not as a performance that would be evaluated but more as a communication. I even tried to think about it as ordinary communication, even though I knew, of course, that it wasn't exactly ordinary. Once you think of a speech as communication, you can think of it in terms of your normal everyday conversation rather than giving a big performance. This nonperformance way of thinking helped me realize that the real objective is to communicate.

"The next step followed rather logically. What I really tried to do was to speak the way I talk. I tried to think of my presentation as a casual conversation with someone I respected.

"My instructor used an exercise that was very effective. He would tell me to forget about giving a speech and to simply talk spontaneously. He and I would talk back and forth in a conversational mode, but I would use the outline notes that I had developed for my speech as a guide. What I found was that I was able to use natural language and to maintain this conversational style as the keynote of my presentation. And then I turned my outline notes into my PowerPoint slides, so I didn't have to hold any reminder notes during the presentation itself.

"Once I got onto this technique, I would practice this conversational style by myself. You find that you never say what you want to say exactly as you prepared it, and this preserves the naturalness of the presentation."

"So now you have no anxiety?" asked Keith.

Helen laughed. "Well," she said, "I still have some anxiety, but I'm able to keep it under control and even use it in a positive way to keep up my enthusiasm and motivation. But most of all I just keep thinking of my presentations as conversations, and this keeps my confidence up. After all, you know I *do* like to talk!"

"Do you think you could help me?" asked Keith.

"Sure," replied Helen. "First let's work on your outline notes, so you're sure of your objective, your structure, and your content. But *do not* write the speech! Then we can use the technique of my instructor, rehearsing the presentation as a conversation between the two of us. After we've done it a couple of times, I'll help you develop your PowerPoint slides and then we'll invite one or two sympathetic friends to join us as we go over it again. You'll see. You'll end up being a pro. It's all in the way you think!"

Of course, this SuperLeadership behavior is well founded in the results of research on the self-fulfilling prophecy: if a person believes something can be done, that belief makes it more likely that it will be done. Perhaps Helen was playing Professor Higgins to Keith's "Eliza." She was creating the positive conditions that were just right for Keith to learn and achieve on his own. In particular, she served as a credible model since she had faced the same difficulties and had succeeded in overcoming them. Also, she provided encouragement and guidance for Keith to accomplish the same result.

S *The SuperLeader creates productive thought patterns by carefully expressing confidence in the follower's ability to extend her present level of competence.*

Most of all, through her expression of confidence in Keith she was helping him to create productive patterns of thinking—new, constructive thought habits. Through a step-by-step process, she was helping Keith to reexamine his beliefs about and images of what public speaking really is. In the end, Keith will likely find himself speaking more effectively to himself (constructive self-talk) as well as to his audience.

Once employees have established constructive patterns of thinking about themselves, these thinking patterns can be extended into their daily work experience. Most notably, it is important that "opportunity thinking" is established. Indeed, even the seemingly most difficult problems contain the seeds of opportunity. When we confidently meet a challenge by turning it into an opportunity, it sets the stage for a whole new innovative breakthrough. Opportunity thinking can be the key to creativity and innovation.

In the end, SuperLeader effectiveness can best be measured by the effectiveness of their followers. Facilitating, encouraging, and supporting self-leadership in individual employees is what Super-Leadership is all about. Primary building blocks for accomplishing this include modeling, goals, rewards, and thought patterns. Leaders that help followers to become capable self-leaders marshal the strength of many, and thus are destined to become SuperLeaders.

Herb Kelleher of Southwest Airlines

Narda Quigley

Herb Kelleher, chairman, president, and CEO of Southwest Airlines, personifies many qualities of SuperLeadership. Kelleher, through his unique blend of wit, energy, and vision, has led Southwest from a humble preflight beginning in 1968 to an established, well-respected company with a unique culture and reputation. But the airline has enjoyed far more than personality and charm. Southwest has had astounding financial success over the last three decades, due in large part to Kelleher's leadership in creating an empowering corporate culture.

 In 2000, Southwest was named in Fortune *magazine as the most admired airline.*

Today, Southwest is America's fourth largest major carrier (in terms of passengers carried) with over 300 jets, 50 million passengers a year, and service to 56 cities across the nation. Profits have exploded by 838 percent in the last decade and the number of passengers carried, airplanes, and employees have all tripled.[1] The company has reported annual profits for an astounding 27 consecutive years, even during the industry-wide downturn of the early 1990s. With its low-cost, high-customer-satisfaction strategy, Southwest has become "the nation's premier shorthaul, point-to-point, low-fare carrier."[2] In addition, Southwest routinely captures customer service awards such as the coveted Triple Crown award (best on-time record, baggage handling, and fewest customer complaints). Southwest is clearly widely respected both in business circles and among savvy, cost-conscious travelers.

KELLEHER: A MODEL OF SUPERLEADERSHIP

Why has this upstart airline enjoyed such dramatic success? Much of the answer lies in the leadership of Herb Kelleher, who has managed to cultivate an empowering corporate culture that has become the hallmark of Southwest through the years. His leadership is characterized by the "introduction of innovative programs, a devotion to employees, and a sharp focus on customer service, all of which have helped create a universally admired corporate culture."[3] The key to Kelleher's leadership success seems to lie in the values he has consistently demonstrated and instilled in the organization—values that are strongly based on employee self-leadership. At Southwest, employees enjoy a refreshing environment that promotes self-leadership in every corner of the company.

Southwest employees pooled their own money on Bosses Day for a $60,000 ad thanking Kelleher "for being a friend, not just a boss."

In fact, Kelleher's name has been synonymous with building a culture of empowerment since the founding of the airline. In 1971 he co-founded Southwest as an intrastate carrier serving three Texas cities with three planes. He fought a series of landmark legal battles during the company's infancy, winning the right to fly within the state of Texas during a time when the airline industry was extensively regulated. These battles gave life to an underdog spirit— the symbol of Southwest's unique brand of self-leadership—that continues to characterize the airline and serves as a foundation upon which the corporate culture is built.[4] As Kelleher stated, "We are the underdog. . . . You always have to be lean, you have to be fit; you always have to remember that there are a lot of great white sharks cruising around looking for dinner, and Southwest would be a very appetizing dinner for many of them."[5] In recent years, a time of great profitability and growth for the airline, Kelleher has made a point of keeping his company's feet on the ground. "The biggest challenge," Kelleher noted, "is that Southwest never forgets the fundamentals of what makes [us] successful. That we don't become spoiled or cocky or complacent or arrogant or forgetful—that is a prime concern."[6]

One of the most notable values that Kelleher has fostered and modeled is the emphasis he has placed on every employee as a valuable resource and human being. He has demonstrated his high regard for employees as valuable self-leading peers. Not only has he gone out of his way to learn their names, he has rolled up his sleeves and chipped in to get the work done. He is widely recognized throughout the company for symbolic acts such as lugging baggage and personally greeting customers. And Southwest employees have reciprocated their appreciation. In one of the more dramatic examples, employees pooled their own money and paid $60,000 for an ad in *USA Today* to thank Kelleher on Bosses Day "for being a friend, not just a boss."

VALUES THAT FOSTER
SELF-LEADERSHIP AT SOUTHWEST

From Kelleher's viewpoint, the "fundamentals" of success entail building a special corporate culture. Three major values characterize the spirit of Southwest's culture that helps instill and guide a sense of self-leadership in all its employees: "luv" (or altruism), fun, and humor. Kelleher believes these three values are what make Southwest unique—and profitable. As he told *Fortune* magazine in 1999, "You can get an airplane. You can get ticket counter space; you can get baggage conveyors.... [But] it's the intangibles that are the hardest thing for a competitor to imitate."

Kelleher uses the airline's culture as a way to empower Southwest's employees. He uses it to pull the airline's employees into the company's mission, instilling within them the three values that only become stronger as they take root and grow within the individuals. By imparting a sense of individual importance in each of Southwest's employees through this spread of its corporate culture, Kelleher is able to empower each individual.

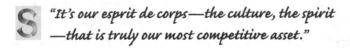

"It's our esprit de corps—the culture, the spirit —that is truly our most competitive asset."

The value of "luv" unifies the employees, who are the heart and soul of Southwest. Southwest is truly a company built from the bottom up; much of the corporate culture revolves around the idea that the employees are there for each other and for the creation of something bigger than any individual: a great airline. As Kelleher explained, his organization is "interested in people who externalize, who focus on other people, who are really motivated to help other people. We are not interested in navel-gazers, regardless of how lint-free their navels are."[7]

In addition to taking such a boldly benevolent stand, Kelleher himself effectively models altruism in the workplace. He sees himself as Southwest's "fireman," the person who does "what no one else wanted to do."[8] Kelleher's own devotion—his luv—for his employees is well known. Part of his luv manifests itself through leadership; the culture is not just about Kelleher's personality and charm. Employees feel empowered and have the opportunity to advance within the airline. As Rita Bailey, director of the company's training arm, explained, "The key to this company is its people. Our focus is on picking the right people, instilling a sense of belonging and the values and culture of the company. Because Southwest promotes so much from within, our programs focus on developing skills for the next level."[9]

Although the airline is 87 percent unionized, it has never had a strike or a layoff. The reason for this extraordinary statistic can be traced directly to Kelleher's SuperLeadership, which is an outgrowth of his genuine concern for his employees. Julius Maldutis, who follows the airline industry for CIBC Oppenheimer, noted, "Herb has built an extraordinary airline that is now self-sustaining, and which is really managed by all the employees."[10]

Kelleher's empowering style seems to manifest itself in the importance he places on luv. The message has certainly hit home with his employees, as Southwest's luv transcends the boundaries of the company. The airline has had an extensive relationship of giving to Ronald McDonald Houses within their city network. Employees do not simply donate money, however; they donate their time. About 25 percent of Southwest's people volunteer some of their time and talent cooking, playing, or in some other way helping in the Ronald McDonald Houses. Clearly, the value that Kelleher has placed on altruism has taken deep root within his employees. The fact that Kelleher's employees go above and beyond what is expected of them is a testament to Kelleher's SuperLeadership.

Two more values are fundamental to understanding the nature of Southwest's culture. Kelleher has worked hard to insure that each employee understands that (1) work should be fun—it can be play—it should be enjoyed, and that (2) work is important and shouldn't be spoiled with too much seriousness. While many companies may talk the same talk, Kelleher has truly walked the walk—and the airline has followed in his footsteps.

Kelleher often models behaviors that support these two values. As J.C. Quick wrote, "Americans create a false dichotomy which says, in effect, 'If it's fun, it can't be work. Or, if it's not fun, then it must be work.'"[11] Kelleher's first value boldly stands out against this dichotomy—he enthusiastically blurs the line between work and play, emphasizing natural rewards. Kelleher himself is a living example of on-the-job enjoyment; his daily energy and enthusiasm for his work are a direct result of his inherent enjoyment of his job. Kelleher is known for fun surprises, such as the time he greeted holiday passengers in an Easter Bunny costume. As he has stated, "If you enjoy what you are doing, then there's no limit to the amount of time you can spend doing it. . . . My enthusiasm is as strong today as it was in 1966 when I started working on Southwest. So it's not a burden, it's not a task, it's not something I'm looking for relief from."[12]

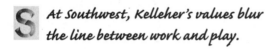

At Southwest, Kelleher's values blur the line between work and play.

Kelleher's infectious enthusiasm is impossible to avoid at Southwest. Part of the reason for that is Southwest's careful selection criterion. Kelleher understands the importance of having people who share his energetic enthusiasm in the workplace. As a result, his recruitment practices actively include things such as searching for people with the right "attitudes." In his own words, "We can train people to do things where skills are concerned. But there is one capability we do not have and that is to change a person's attitude. So, we prefer an unskilled person with a good attitude rather than a highly skilled person with a bad attitude. We take people who come out of highly structured, hierarchical, dictatorial corporate environments if they have the attitude potential. . . . When we have them here for a while, they learn how to relax . . . and let their real selves come out."[13]

The value Kelleher places on enthusiasm appears to help Southwest's employees to be better able to lead themselves. Their enthusiasm has them looking at how they can go above and beyond the call of duty. At Southwest, people have a higher potential for working with their hearts and excelling with the motivation and spirit derived from the cultural values.

Kelleher also conducts himself in accordance with Southwest's third value, which says that work should not be spoiled with seriousness. In addition to his characteristic energy and enthusiasm, the successful CEO goes about his daily tasks with an outrageous sense of humor, which in turn trickles down through the culture of the airline. For example, in the early 1990s Southwest began painting jets with an unusual black-and-white pattern that closely resembled whale coloration. Then-CEO Bob Crandall of American Airlines, who has enjoyed a jocular relationship with Kelleher over the years, asked Kelleher what he was going to do with all the whale droppings from Southwest's freshly painted "Shamu One." Kelleher, without missing a beat, responded to the Rhode Island native, "I'm going to turn it into chocolate mousse and feed it to the Yankees from Rhode Island." Sure enough, the next day, Kelleher followed up by delivering a tub of chocolate mousse to Crandall's office with a king-sized Shamu spoon.[14]

Southwest's employees have taken Kelleher's humorous nature and made it their own. Southwest is known for the antics of its unconventional, humorous employees, who work to give each passenger a unique, fun experience on the way to their destinations. Examples of constructive humor in the workplace abound at the airline. When the new corporate headquarters at Love Field in Dallas was completed, the entire staff moved into the new facility—all, that is, except the dispatchers. The dispatchers' mock outrage began an amusing parody of a war. Employees petitioned not to have the dispatchers come over at all for the open house at the new headquarters. The dispatchers, in turn, arrived early and set up valet parking exclusively for themselves. To retaliate, the employees in the new headquarters building got together and "decorated" the dispatchers' offices with decaying flowers with wilted heads. The dispatchers then sent a letter outlining their bitter resolve to carry on the struggle forever.[15] As Quick explained, "Employees place [the shenanigans] in perspective, realizing that antics are the lubricant that greases the engine of the business."[16] Clearly, Kelleher has set the standard for humor and models it effectively in the Southwest workplace. His employees feel empowered enough to relax and have fun with each other.

Kelleher understands, however, the distinction between positive, tension-releasing or team-building humor and negative, offensive or destructive humor. Humor always must be buttressed by the value of tolerance: in Kelleher's words, "Tolerance for human beings, their peculiarities and eccentricities and their differences, is very important."[17] This emphasis on tolerance helps ensure that the type of humor at Southwest does not exclude people or create joy at the expense of others.

BEYOND THE LEADER: THE CHALLENGE
OF SUSTAINING SELF-LEADERSHIP

Kelleher trusts that his modeling of the behaviors of fun, humor, and altruism will trickle down through the corporate culture to his employees. A key for the airline, up until now, has been to select the people who have the potential to let loose and have a good time at work. The success of the last decade, however, and Kelleher's increasing age, bring two new challenges to the forefront. The near-tripling of the airline's workforce in the last ten years is gradually making it harder "to sustain the close-knit culture credited with much of the company's success."[18] Kelleher himself acknowledges this; unlike competitors obsessing over their rivals' every move, Southwest's greatest challenge comes from within, he has said. "Workplace consultants have long worried that one of the carrier's most important competitive advantages, its team-oriented and fun-loving culture, would slowly disintegrate as the airline quadrupled in size and spread far beyond Dallas."[19] In addition, Kelleher was diagnosed with prostate cancer in 1999, raising the question of what direction Southwest will take when he is no longer actively in the picture.

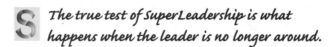

S The true test of SuperLeadership is what
happens when the leader is no longer around.

The true test of a SuperLeader's effectiveness in leading people to lead themselves is what happens when the leader is out of the picture. Will Southwest's prized culture live on in the spirit of its employees after Kelleher's personality and wit are no longer at the helm? There has been a good deal of speculation on this topic. As management consultant Ed Lawler, director of the Center for Effective Organizations, has said, "One of the issues that comes up is how much of [Southwest's] culture is independent of their leader. . . . That still remains something to be proven."[20] With or without Kelleher at the helm, though, some observers expect Southwest "to profitably carry on with its miserly ways.' From the very beginning, they've always done their own thing,' said Ed Perkins, consumer advocate with the American Society of Travel Agents."[21] While there is a fair amount of evidence that Kelleher is indeed a SuperLeader, the true nature of his leadership ability should become crystal clear when he retires.

9 Leading Teams to Self-Leadership

"**BILL! CONTACT CHADSMITH LTD.** about the chip order that they have not filled yet and let them know that they either need to get on this or we will drop them as a supplier. Then check back with me for further instructions. Frankly, I think your team has been too lax with them and I want to get things moving," Ann Faber, the newly hired team leader curtly directed Bill, one of the Blue Team members. "And we need it now, so I want you to drop everything and get on this!" Uncharacteristically, Bill didn't say a word, even though he knew the order had been shipped by FedEx that morning. He simply quietly walked away with an irritated look on his face.

"Take it easy," a quiet voice suggested to Ann after Bill had left. Ann turned to see Blake Reed, another team leader, standing near her with a friendly smile on his face. "You're pressing too hard, Ann. The Blue Team is very good and they can handle this themselves. I think you're over-managing a bit."

"Pardon me?" Ann looked genuinely surprised. "I'm just trying to clear up a problem before it gets out of control. The order is already a week late and I thought it was my job to make sure things don't happen like this in my work teams."

"Haven't you gotten the word yet? We don't lead our teams that way around here. I've noticed you supervising your teams very closely since you came on board last week, and sometimes you're pretty harsh. We are committed to getting our team members to learn how to manage themselves in this organization. A key part of our job is to help create a system in which all team members see themselves as an important resource and a self-manager. Bill and the other team members know the order is late and they are working on it. In fact you could learn a lot from them if you ask them what's going on."

Ann still looked confused. She had just taken her new position with Arlington Technology after serving as a team leader with Astin Semiconductor for the last three years. Astin also relied on work teams but Ann had always supervised members fairly closely in order to get the work out. She recalled a colleague at Astin grinning when he heard she had accepted a position with Arlington. He had said, "You may be in for a shock—they operate their team system very differently over there." Ann had wondered what he meant, but wasn't too concerned because she knew that Arlington was the best in the industry and she felt her ability to lead would be well rewarded in such a strong company. Now it suddenly occurred to her that maybe she had a lot to learn about leadership, at least in the team system at Arlington Technology.

What is the real job of a leader, especially a team leader? Is it more important to get the work out now, or to contribute to the development of team members so that they can lead themselves? What is your own approach when *you* are in the position of leading a team? Effective self-leadership systems require more than resources and psychological support provided by the organization and its culture. Systems are needed that will facilitate rather than retard self-leadership. Self-managing teams are perhaps the most important of various systems available for supporting the practice of SuperLeadership. In fact, when U.S. companies speak of "empowerment" it's usually implemented through some form of self-managing teams.

SELF-MANAGING TEAMS: SOME BACKGROUND

Self-managing teams had a slow start in the United States. Eventually, media interest helped—now teams are recognized as an important organization design feature and used in most major industries.

Early dramatic, widely publicized successes with the team approach such as the GM-Toyota joint venture in Fremont, California, were instructive to the U.S. automotive industry and to organizations in general. In fact, one of the more public issues of the GM-UAW negotiations in the late 1980s was GM's desire to move the total corporation to the team concept.

The idea and interest in teams has been around for a long time. Years ago, top-management teams were already important to Tom Watson, Jr., former CEO of IBM. "My most important contribution to IBM was my ability to pick strong and intelligent men and then hold the team together. . . . I knew I couldn't match all of them intellectually, but I thought that if I used fully every capability that I had, I could stay even with them."[1]

There are a wide variety of types of teams, including manufacturing teams, service teams, product teams, cross-functional teams, top-executive teams, ad hoc teams, and even virtual teams. In today's fast moving, information-rich environment, teams require a good deal of self-leadership to function correctly.

 One of the prominent indicators of a self-leadership culture is the presence of quite a few teams.

Like many Americans, David Packard, cofounder of Hewlett-Packard, learned respect for teams through his athletic experiences. "I liked basketball and track," he recalls. "You learn a lot of things in athletics and they're very important in your later career. . . . You . . . develop a sense of the importance of teamwork . . . whatever you do."[2]

But this sense of teamwork, now ingrained in most Americans as they grow up, has been extensively adapted to the workplace. Consider the case of Consolidated Diesel, an engine manufacturing plant located in Whitakers, N.C.[3]

According to the folks at Consolidated, "Teamwork is the Engine" that assures success at their 20-year-old engine manufacturing plant. Since the beginning, the plant has relied on what they call a "team-based system" where people have a large say in how they go about their work.

The company has created a special culture that involves listening to its employees and involving them in solving problems in the plant.

According to Jim Lyons, general manager, " ... the fact that it's the team's plan, and not a plan dictated by management, means everything. . . . The teams will make it work."

Richard Strawbridge, an 11-year veteran employee, elaborates: "The teams solve a lot of our problems," says Strawbridge. "When I came here I realized that in other places where I had worked, decisions had been made for me. Here I'm required to be involved in the decision-making process."

"When good people are given good information," says Lyons, "they typically make good decisions."

Perhaps the most important point about the Consolidated plant is the sustainability of the team system. For over 20 years, the team system has contributed to the achievement of an extraordinary level of performance.

SELF-MANAGING TEAMS IN ACTION

One of the most interesting aspects of our research program over the past 20 years has been our direct observations of self-managing teams. In an early experience, we were involved with a particular manufacturing plant that was among the earliest sites in the U.S. to adopt self-managing teams. Most of the early applications of self-managed teams were in manufacturing plants.

Hundreds of manufacturing plants have now used some derivative of an empowered team approach. More recently, a wide variety of nonmanufacturing organizations have relied on some variation of this approach, ranging from insurance firms to financial investment firms to high-tech virtual organizations. These work groups, often called "self-managed" or "self-directed" teams, are mainly characterized by an attempt to create a high degree of decision-making autonomy and behavioral control at the work-group level. Consequently, a much greater emphasis is placed on control from within rather than from outside the group. There has been some debate about whether these teams are established to improve productivity or simply the quality of the employee's work life, but it seems clear that management decision makers have implicit (if not explicit) goals of improved productivity, better-quality products, reduced conflict, or all three.

Researchers have often been restricted from studying organizations that use the team approach, and sometimes when they have been given access it is with the proviso that there be no publicity or writing about it. As a result, the research published about self-managing teams tends to lag actual practice in organizations. We have been fortunate to have open access to a variety of organizations using self-managing teamwork systems. One such organization was a manufacturing plant with a team system that had been in place for several years. Since most early work with self-managing teams originated in manufacturing sites, we will describe this plant in some detail as a foundational example of self-managed teams in practice.

Self-Managing Teams in a Manufacturing Operation

The plant we studied was a nonunionized small-parts plant owned by General Motors, located in the southern part of the United States. It employed approximately 320 workers. The plant was established in the early 1970s and was organized from the very beginning according to a self-managing team concept. The technology used in the plant can be described as small-parts production or assembly, and it is generally based on a type of assembly-line system. Each work group was assigned a system of closely related tasks, many of which were small assembly-line operations. Teams were generally distinct from each other, both physically and by in-process inventory buffers.

The organizational structure had three distinct hierarchical levels. Upper plant management (called the support team) handled many traditional plant-management responsibilities (for example, planning overall plant production schedules, dealing with client firms, and so on). The support team was also formally responsible for the supervision of coordinators. The support team generally played a supportive rather than directive role in the plant's operation and its attempts to operate as a team. The work-team coordinators—external leaders who had overall responsibility for one or more teams—occupied the next hierarchical level. The final level was the self-managing work teams themselves. The size of the teams ranged from approximately three to nineteen members, although most included eight to twelve. Within each team, an elected team leader also had leadership responsibilities and received higher pay than other group members. For the most part, this individual did the same physical work as the other employees.

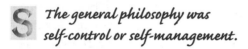

S *The general philosophy was self-control or self-management.*

The work system placed more responsibility on employees than in typical manufacturing environments. The general philosophy was self-control or self-management. Work teams were assigned a wide range of tasks and responsibilities, including preparation of an annual budget, keeping records of the hours they worked, recording quality-control statistics (subject to audit), making intragroup job assignments, and participating in assessment of the job performance of other team members. Teams engaged in various problem-solving activities that included scheduling, equipment, and process problems, as well as group-member behaviors like absenteeism. Weekly scheduled and ad hoc meetings served as problem-solving forums in which such issues were addressed.

Scheduled weekly meetings were typically held away from the production area. Teams were trained in conducting meetings and in group problem solving. Problems were frequently raised for open discussion during these meetings. Usually the elected team leader would organize and conduct the meeting, but other team members were provided with the opportunity to speak freely. The external coordinator or members of the support team were often invited to work with the self-managing team in dealing with specific issues and problems, but did not attend on a routine basis. A coordinator might attend a team meeting, for example, to help members work out a particularly difficult quality-control problem. Our observations of a number of these meetings revealed a relatively sophisticated level of discussion and problem solving (that is, in terms of the technical nature of the discussions and their persistent emphasis on reaching a solution), which focused on improving work performance as well as on the various concerns of individual team members.

The pay system at the plant was based on the expertise level of employees. The level of pay for an individual employee was based on the number of tasks he or she could competently perform. When employees felt they had mastered a given job, they were tested on that job. In order to reach the highest pay level, an employee had to learn all of the jobs of two work groups. This pay system was similar to those used in other early team applications, including a pet-foods plant studied by Richard E. Walton and a paint-production plant studied by Ernesto J. Poza and M. Lynne Markus.[4]

Another distinguishing characteristic of this work system was its noticeable lack of status symbols. The plant manager's office, for example, could be and frequently was used for team meetings without advance permission. There was no assigned parking and a single cafeteria was used by all employees.

Self-Managing Communication

Many of the self-management activities took place during team meetings, which normally served as problem-solving forums. Each team had at least one regularly scheduled half-hour team meeting each week. In addition, special meetings were called to deal with specific problems. All meetings were held on company time, and employees were paid their regular wages while attending.

These team meetings proved to be a rich source of information about the culture of the plant. We attended many of both the routine and special meetings over several weeks. To preserve normal conditions, we did not record conversations but instead took careful notes. In our previous research we had become skilled at systematically categorizing verbal behavior in organizational situations. It was only natural, therefore, that we should give special attention to the nature of the conversations within these self-managed work teams

We noted a rich array of types of communication exchanged between team members during our visits including frequent use of:

▶ Praise and compliments.

▶ Corrective feedback, or criticisms.

▶ Task assignments.

▶ Work scheduling.

▶ Production goal setting and performance feedback.

▶ Routine announcements.

▶ Problem solving.

▶ Discussion of communication problems.

▶ Performance evaluations.

▶ Other general team issues.

For example, compliments, thanks and praise were exchanged face-to-face in response to a useful or helpful action—"Bobby, thanks for all your help with the inspection of the machine last night." Or perhaps during a meeting a member might announce, "We owe a special thanks to Emily for making sure that the materials were ready last Monday. We would have had to shut down if she hadn't looked ahead and gotten what we needed."

We also observed corrective feedback, or criticisms. An especially dramatic incident at a regular team meeting was initiated by the team leader: "Jerry, we want to talk to you now about your absenteeism." He then went on to recount Jerry's record of absenteeism and the dates he had been absent. After allowing Jerry to respond, the team leader went on to talk about the negative effect of absenteeism on the other team members and on team performance. He stated unambiguously that Jerry's absences were "unacceptable. We won't allow it to continue." He said that if he were absent one more time, Jerry would face a formal disciplinary charge that would be entered into the record. The team leader concluded by asking Jerry about his intentions. Jerry replied, "I guess I've been absent about as much as I can get away with. I guess I better come to work."

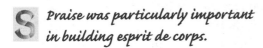

S *Praise was particularly important in building esprit de corps.*

Much of the communication centered on special problems. For instance, we observed an interesting incident revolving around the solution of a quality problem. A meeting had been called by a coordinator to discuss a certain quality deficiency. Four members from two different teams were present with the coordinator and a quality-control technician. The coordinator presented the problem, citing statistics that showed a gradual rise in the reject rate over several weeks. He asked, "What's the problem? What can we do to correct it?"

From our viewpoint, the meeting started slowly. No one had an immediate solution. But the coordinator was patient and he listened carefully, encouraging the workers when they spoke. After five minutes, the meeting seemed to become more productive. Over the next half-hour, several causes of the problem were suggested and several "fixes" were proposed. Near the end, the group listed the proposed solutions according to ease of implementation and agreed to begin applying them in an attempt to eliminate the problem. Afterward, we asked the coordinator whether he had actually learned anything new or was just going through the motions for the sake of participation. "Sure," he replied. "I wasn't aware of many of the ideas they brought out. But most of all, they've now taken it on as their problem, and they will do whatever has to be done to solve it."

S *The teams devoted much of their efforts to solving quality problems.*

Team communication provided a rich indication of both attitudes and behavior in the plant. While some of it reflected self-concern and was sometimes trivial, in general the organizational commitment and motivation of these employees were among the highest we had observed.

If any executive is asked what his major problem is, the chances are good that the reply would be something like this: "Communication. Our communication is not what it should be. We just never seem to have the right information at the right place at the right time." Inadequate communication often means inadequate information sharing. Too often the problem has been the result of a policy of secrecy: tell employees only what they need to know to do their jobs. Consequently, employees often don't really have all the information needed to perform the job.

At the plant a strong sharing philosophy prevailed. Management's viewpoint seemed to be to share virtually all information that was not considered personal. As a result we found a climate of openness that was virtually unprecedented in our previous experience. And this information sharing provided a basis for employees to engage in proactive problem solving that enabled them to discover and correct problems at a relatively early stage.

Management's role was not to *directly* provide motivation and discipline to individual employees. Instead, management created a climate in which motivation and discipline came mainly from within the individual employees and their team members. In our opinion this is a most effective form of motivation, and gets translated into bottom-line productivity.

We do not wish to leave the impression that the plant was a model of tranquility and harmony. On the contrary, in this plant as well as in several other self-managed team settings we have studied, interactions between members of the self-managing teams were sometimes tough and intense. We observed emotional conflict, but the prevailing mode seemed to be to deal with the conflict openly and directly. Overall, the level of motivation and commitment was high.

LEADING SELF-MANAGING TEAMS

Much of the leadership in the team system was conducted by the coordinators, the external leaders of the self-managing teams. We think of coordinators as a type of SuperLeader—they lead teams to lead themselves.

We observed coordinators encouraging teams to engage in self-leadership behaviors such as self-observation, self-evaluation, and self-problem-solving. For example, we observed a coordinator encourage a young production worker who had discovered a quality problem to solve the quality defect on his own, and save the plant a great deal of cost in the process.

We also observed coordinators conducting role-playing exercises with elected team leaders—a form of rehearsal—and encouraging groups to evaluate themselves and to give both positive and negative feedback within the team. In the instance mentioned earlier, where a team conducted a formal reprimand of a team member during a team meeting for excessive absenteeism, the coordinator had encouraged this confrontation and worked with team members in rehearsing approaches for the meeting. Our subsequent direct observation revealed a very effective meeting.

Consistent with the SuperLeadership perspective, we observed a notable absence of direct commands or instructions from the coordinators to the teams. However, questions (an important tool of guided participation) were used with great frequency. "What is a reasonable scrap rate to shoot for?" (facilitating self-goal-setting); "What will you say to Bill about his absenteeism?" (encouraging rehearsal); "Do you think you can do it?" (eliciting high self-expectation). In one instance an employee informed his coordinator that a piece of equipment had been damaged and asked the coordinator what he should do. The coordinator responded by asking, "What do you think should be done?" After a moment of reflection, the employee indicated what he thought would be appropriate and, with the coordinator's encouragement and reinforcement, proceeded with the repair according to his own plan.

Many other coordinator behaviors had self-leadership implications. A special team meeting might be suggested by a coordinator to solve a difficult quality or process problem, and the meeting would be carried out by the team itself. Coordinators also used a variety of practical behaviors more typical of leaders in general, such as communicating between work groups and management and using positive verbal reward. Overall, we observed a general pattern of behavior that was quite different from our previous experiences in more traditional production plants.

 The underlying theme of leadership practice was for the coordinators to influence team members to do it themselves.

A list of relevant leadership behaviors derived from our research at the plant is provided in the following table. This list can serve as a beginning guide for identifying appropriate leader behavior for facilitating team performance.

Some of the leadership behaviors found in this research are similar to those in the existing leadership literature: communicating between a work group and management, and between work groups, helping to assure that work groups have the equipment and supplies they need, training inexperienced employees, and so on. However, a fundamental difference does exist in how leadership functions are carried out, especially in terms of the shift in the source of control from the leader to the follower. The uniqueness of the self-managed team leader's role lies in the commitment to the philosophy that the team should successfully complete necessary leadership functions for itself. The dominant role of the external leader, then, is SuperLeadership—to lead others to lead themselves. This is quite different from the traditional role of the leader as the one holding all the power and initiative to influence others.

In terms of performance, our conversations with corporate officials indicated productivity gains significantly greater than 20 percent when compared to other plants of the same technology using more traditional management methods. Our discussions with

Leader Behavior	Description
Trains experienced employees	Leader trains group members on various group jobs.
Encourages group problem solving	Leader encourages group to solve its own problems.
Encourages within-group job assignments	Leader encourages the group to assign tasks to its members on its own.
Encourages flexible task boundaries	Leader encourages group to be flexible in its work (i.e., to do whatever needs to be done that the work group is capable of).
Positive verbal reward	Leader verbally rewards (i.e., praises) group for desirable performance.
Constructive corrective feedback	Leader constructively provides feedback to the team on where and how it might improve.
Goal setting	Leader facilitates performance goals for the work group.
Expectation of group performance	Leader expects high group performance.
Communicates production schedule	Leader communicates to the group about plant production schedule (including any changes).
Works alongside employees	Leader physically works with group members to help them do their work.
Truthfulness	Leader communicates in a way that is truthful and believable to group members.
Encourages self-reward	Leader encourages work group to be self-reinforcing of high group performance.
Encourages self-criticism	Leader encourages work group to be constructively self-critical of low group performance.
Encourages self-observation/ evaluation	Leader encourages work group to monitor, be aware of, and evaluate level of performance.
Encourages rehearsal	Leader encourages work group to go over an activity and "think it through" before actually performing the activity.
Communicates to/ from management	Leader communicates group views to upper management (i.e., supports group) and management views to the group.

(continued)

Leader Behavior	Description
Facilitates equipment/supplies	Leader facilitates obtaining equipment and supplies for the work group.
Communicates between groups	Leader communicates group views to and from other groups.
Encourages within-group communication	Leader encourages open communication among group members, including the exchange of information for learning new jobs.

management also revealed similar positive comparisons regarding quality, turnover, and worker satisfaction. For example, in response to a question about turnover, a manager in the plant counted on the fingers of one hand the employees who had chosen to leave.

 Officials indicated productivity gains "significantly greater than 20 percent."

After our research in this remarkable plant we went on to study teams in many industries, including paper production, insurance, energy production, financial services, communications, warehousing, aircraft engine design and testing, automobile, and computer components, among many others. These organizations ranged from small firms to *Fortune* 500 companies.

Given the important role played by manufacturing firms in pioneering the use of self-managing teams, the small-parts plant we reviewed above provides a good foundational view. This case provides a rich source of learning for a setting in which people work in the same physical location and must work together to accomplish their tasks. On the other hand, the knowledge-based high-tech world of the 21st century poses special challenges for teams. Perhaps the most striking evolution that now confronts many organizations is the emergence of virtual working relationships and, more specific to this discussion, virtual teams.

As an example, one large multinational corporation, referred to by the pseudonym Xeon, discovered a number of challenges in working with a structure based on virtual teams.[5] A $50 billion company operating in over 70 countries, Xeon introduced virtual teams to encourage collaboration within and between its business units, as well as contractors and partners in joint ventures. Virtual teamwork was established with the aid of powerful computers equipped for videoconferencing, plus scanning and multimedia e-mail and groupware.

S *"Broadband communication will enhance the richness of distant collaboration . . . [especially] the possibilities of virtual teaming."*
—Philip Evans & Thomas S. Wurster[6]

The advanced technology made available within the organization facilitated communication, collaboration, and knowledge-sharing among employees located around the world. It also changed the nature of work within the organization in a variety of ways. For example, documents were shared on-line including contracts, plans, presentations, and engineering drawings. Further, temporary task-based teams involving specialists across diverse settings were able to combine expertise and solve problems in remote locations. Also, senior management input and authority were found to be more potent in remote sites when relying on the variety of new technologies, especially videoconferencing, than when relying on more traditional communications channels such as telephones and the mail.

In total, the advanced technology and virtual teaming at Xeon introduced a number of pervasive changes in the way tasks were performed and the way employees experienced their work. Throughout the process, many challenges such as hierarchical norms and cultural differences across geographical settings posed difficulties for optimal interaction and collaboration. Perhaps the biggest challenge for optimal performance with the virtual team system centered on the issue of trust. Members of temporary virtual teams brought together to solve significant problems had to depend on collective knowledge and diverse skills of other members with whom they had little or no history.

This was a difficult hurdle for many employees to cross. As a result, virtual team members went out of their way to make face-to-face contact with others in order to build mutual confidence and a more developed relationship. When this was not feasible, many employees found it very difficult to open up and share concerns or feelings they had related to the work, and were often reluctant to share information and knowledge, especially when it was of a more personal nature. Ultimately it became clear that the technology that made communication and knowledge-sharing possible was not adequate to meet more human needs for feeling confidence and trust in others.

> *In the knowledge-based economy, workers will be valued for their ability to create, judge, imagine, and build relationships.*[7]

A primary lesson from the experience of Xeon is that virtual teams based on the impressive technology of the information age provide tremendous opportunities but cannot eliminate the need, at least yet, for more basic human interaction—especially face-to-face communication in the same location. And an even more fundamental lesson is that the new types of teams found in the 21st century will encounter many significant challenges of an unprecedented nature. Indeed, effective team SuperLeadership—leading teams to lead themselves—in the information age will require the insights and knowledge of many in order to meet these new challenges.

Joe Paterno and Phil Jackson— SuperLeadership in Sports

One of the more interesting arenas for studying leadership is found in sports teams. In this profile we focus on two of the most fascinating and effective team coaches in history—Joe Paterno and Phil Jackson. Not only have these two leaders enjoyed remarkable success but they have demonstrated a complex blend of different types of leadership that distinguish them from the typical athletic coach.

JOE PATERNO

By any standard, Joseph Vincent Paterno has reached the pinnacle of success in American college football. As head coach at Penn State, Paterno is one of football's all-time winningest coaches. But Paterno is respected for his philosophy and opinions as well as for his coaching achievements. Sometimes he seems prouder of the percentage of Penn State athletes who graduate than of his own winning percentage.

Many leaders struggle with the challenge of leading the way they think they *should* versus their own natural style. Paterno is no exception. In a personal interview,[1] we found Coach Paterno to have a special ability to be introspective about this dilemma of over-control and under-control. "It's difficult," he candidly admits, "for me to handle people in the way I think they want to be handled . . . because I have a tendency to want *complete* control. . . . In the early part of my career . . . I would plot every offensive and defensive move we would use in a ball game, and try to devise the game plan by myself. . . . I felt that I had to have input on everything that went on, every minute of the day and every day of the week."[2]

Paterno also recognizes the benefits of getting others involved in the action—especially assistant coaches. According to Joe, "I'm cognizant that people will not work two extra hours at the film projector if they're going to come in the next day and be told exactly what to do . . . that's not going to work. . . . You destroy any ingenuity . . . any satisfaction they get out of the job itself. I'm aware of that . . . I have to fight like hell to constantly remind myself of it."

On the practice field, Paterno is a well-known "screamer," cajoling his players to higher intensity. A casual observer would classify Paterno as a classic Strongman leader. But behind the scenes, Paterno also reaches out in a unique way to his players. For example, in the early 90s Joe started meeting informally with a group of representatives from the players each Wednesday morning at 7:15 in a cafeteria for "Java with Joe." They have an open discussion of what is happening on the team and why.

Paterno started these meetings after a frustrating 1992 season that ended with five defeats, a new low in Paterno's coaching career. "I thought I had lost the squad,"[3] said Paterno. He realized he needed a new avenue of communication with today's new breed of player. Paterno characterized these meetings as " ... the culmination of talking and getting things out in the open, and understanding we're all in this together." In these meetings Paterno seemed to behave like a SuperLeader, asking, "What's going on? Is there something you want me to address with the coaches? How do you feel?" In the end, the team responded with an undefeated season in 1994 capped by a victory in the Rose Bowl.

> *They have open discussions of what's happening and why.*

This type of behavior has a way of catching on without the players really realizing it. At the time, senior All-American quarterback Kerry Collins was quoted as saying, "It's funny, I'll be talking to people and I'll start saying things that he has said for four years. And I'll think, 'What am I doing?'"[4]

According to Paterno, having the opportunity to fail—making mistakes—is part of the learning process. "You can't grow [if you don't make mistakes]. ... I've got to give them a chance to do some things [on their own]." Paterno recognizes the value of mistakes in his own development, saying his former coach " ... allowed me to make a lot of mistakes. ... Many times, I would go in there with the 'greatest idea in the world' [when] it may have been tried three different times [and] it didn't work. ... I do the same thing. ... [An assistant coach] will come in with a 'great idea' ... I saw the same thing 12 years ago. ... [They] do some things I'm sure are not going to work." He clearly has a SuperLeader perspective: "Your assistant coaches will only grow if you allow them to try new things."[5]

Joe Paterno[6]

Joe Paterno, head football coach at Penn State University, has achieved a remarkable record of performance on and off the field. No college football coach in the history of the sport has won more postseason bowl games than Paterno. He is the only man to win four New Year's Day bowl games—the Rose, Sugar, Cotton, and Orange Bowls. And, he is closing in on one of the game's most treasured records. With over 300 lifetime victories he is close to breaking Bear Bryant's lifetime victories record.

Paterno's record includes two National Championships, five undefeated, untied teams, 20 finishes in the top ten of the national rankings, and four "coach of the year" awards. Since 1950, when Paterno came on board as assistant coach, Penn State has a winning percentage of .759, the best of any team in college football.

As a head coach, he has had at least one first-team All-American 31 times, 14 Hall of Fame Scholar-Athletes, 21 first-team Academic All-Americans, and 17 NCAA postgraduate scholarship winners. More than 225 former players have made it to the National Football League—25 of them first-round draft choices.

Yet, for all the accomplishments on the field, one sports columnist observed, "From the perspective of meaningful contributions to society, the least important thing Joe Paterno does is coach football." He and his family have a lifetime giving record to Penn State of more than $4 million. His support of the university has been long-standing and exceptional.

He has often said he measures his success not by athletic prowess, but by the number of players who become productive citizens and make a contribution to society.

Phil Jackson

Phil Jackson achieved the pinnacle of the professional basketball profession by achieving a lofty .738 regular season winning percentage in nine seasons as head coach of the Chicago Bulls, best in NBA history. His playoff winning percentage at the Bulls was .730, leading to six championships. He has continued his winning ways as head coach of the Los Angeles Lakers, winning the NBA championship in 2000.

Jackson earned the NBA Coach of the Year award in 1996 as his team won a league-record 72 games during the regular season, and its fourth NBA title.

Part of his ability as a coach is derived from his experience as a player in the 1970s, where he was a key figure in the New York Knicks' unselfish, team-oriented style of play, leading to a championship in 1973. As a coach, the hallmark of his teams has been his emphasis on the basics of defense and teamwork.

Jackson is also an author, publishing *Maverick* (1975) and *Sacred Hoops: Spiritual Lessons of a Hardwood Warrior* (1995). Most of all he is known for his unusual style of coaching, which places a high degree of self-responsibility on the players.

Paterno seems to be destined to fight with himself over the classic dilemma between his natural "hands-on" activist, Strongman leadership style, and the behaviors required of a SuperLeader. This seems to be a conflict between his emotional self, which has a strong desire to control—perhaps overcontrol—the situation, versus his intellectual self, which realizes the necessity and benefit of providing more opportunity for his assistant coaches. The "natural" self says, "Hey, I gotta get in there and do it myself" while the intellectual self says, "I have to stand back and give them an opportunity to do it." In the end, he says, the important thing "is still keeping control, but knowing when you don't have to have control."

Paterno remains an intriguing combination of many of the leader behaviors we have described in this book: practice-field Strongman, university Visionary, and behind-the-scenes SuperLeader. Perhaps it is his complexity that makes him so appealing.

PHIL JACKSON

If you look at the record it's impossible to ignore the remarkable achievements of Phil Jackson as coach of the NBA champions Chicago Bulls and Los Angeles Lakers. But when you try to get past the statistics and understand Jackson as leader, you realize what an unusual coach he is. He is complex and sometimes seemingly contradictory in his leadership; a man who mixes elements of Strongman, Visionary Hero, and SuperLeadership. Whatever it is, his leadership has been accepted by the prima donna players of two teams and has achieved that Holy Grail of professional sports, championships.

In an era where the stereotypical image of a coach is screaming at players, Jackson leads with a different philosophy. In an introspective mood, he shared some of his views about coaching and leading with Bob Costas,[7] the sports announcer. Jackson believes in putting the spotlight on the players, not on himself. Most of all in a SuperLeader mode, he talked about focusing on the players:" ...You have to make it the best possible situation for the players, so that they can get *themselves* to the position [to win]." He stated further, "It is more about establishing [their] belief in themselves."

Jackson has a clear philosophy about control. "The biggest thing about talent is that you don't have too much control ... [don't] take too much of the fame ... or the blame ... for *their* success." Writing in the *New York Times*, David Shields claimed that Jackson's aim is to "yield control at a superficial level in order to regain it at a more profound level, where players 'become policemen of themselves.'"[8]

Shields called Jackson "The Good Father" because of the special way he relates to players. Veteran Lakers player John Salley said of Jackson, "With Phil, it's 'You're a man, I'm a man. I'm going to help you be a better man.'"

In contrast to most coaches, Jackson seldom calls plays on the court. According to Shields, "He is an authority figure whose authority derives from his strategic willingness to deconstruct that authority." June Jackson, his wife, says that "Sometimes he keeps things moving by not doing anything. With Phil, there's a flowing rather than a forcing." Perhaps the most striking difference between Jackson and other coaches is his decorum during a game. While most coaches are seen intensely shouting directions and commands (often on deaf ears!), Jackson is most often seen sitting on the bench, arms folded, yet keenly observing the flow of the game.

One of the more revealing incidents is Jackson's response to a situation where Chicago player Scottie Pippen refused to enter a playoff game with 1.8 seconds to go. After the game, Jackson's response, in a classic SuperLeadership style, was to put the monkey on the players' backs. He closed the locker room and said, "What happened has hurt us. Now you have to work this out. You've got two minutes to get together, to talk softly among yourselves." Later, he described this incident as one where he . . . let the team come up with its own solutions.

 "You guys are out on the floor. . . . Don't be afraid to come to me and tell me what you see."
— **Phil Jackson, attributed by player Brian Shaw**

Many leadership pundits believe that sports coaches in particular need to be authoritarian and directive in order to control emotional, self-centered athletes. The classic stereotype is the coach shouting and gesturing, with an occasional toss of a chair across the court. Sports teams are, in fact, the last bastion of Strongman leadership, where the coach has the ultimate authority to express his power without restraint. Jackson stands in stark contrast to this Strongman model, through his emphasis on player self-leadership and self-motivation. If only because of his remarkable record of achievement, his special form of leadership can serve as a model of a different way of leading teams.

10 Leading Organizational Cultures to Self-Leadership

THURSDAY EVENING, 7:30 P.M. In his office on the seventh floor, Michael G. Smith, new CEO of Avant-Garde Computer, Inc. (AGC), examines the last sales report. The message is depressing: sales have leveled off in the past year. AGC is a small, innovative young company located in Silicon Valley. Founded eight years ago, AGC specializes in engineering graphics design software. The founder, an engineer himself, had successfully marketed two highly specialized software packages for mechanical and electronic design.

The founder (now retired) depended heavily on the two chief engineers who now head the two main divisions of the company. Each is considered to be a brilliant technician. Both engineers are deeply experienced and firmly committed to the present strategy of mechanical and electronic design graphics. Further, both of them are known as "autocrats" who keep a firm hand on the younger engineers within their divisions. They don't believe in delegating decisions. For the last three years, turnover among the younger engineers has been increasing. Michael Smith knows from transcripts of exit interviews that most of them are leaving because of the chief engineers' detailed control over their activities.

Two years ago the need for capital became acute, so the founder sold AGC to a very large multinational corporation. Now, Michael Smith has been appointed CEO by the parent corporation. He recognizes the difficulty of AGC's current situation but he believes a change of strategy can revive the company. His strategy would be to broaden AGC's market by marketing and servicing the software through the Internet. He foresees, however, that AGC's chief engineers would not be thrilled by his view of the future, since they are consumed by the elegance of the design of the software itself and seem to have blind spots in terms of how the products might be brought to market.

Smith believes AGC can survive only if the software is adapted to include user-friendly interfaces to the Internet. Also, he needs to do something about the turnover of the younger engineers. Quite honestly, he really does not know how to introduce these major strategic changes without losing the valuable experience of the two chief engineers. Smith recognizes that AGC will need to empower the younger engineers in the ranks in order to implement this new strategy. He clearly recognizes the need for a cultural change. Now his challenge is to effectively facilitate such a change to enable the organization to meet its current needs, which differ from those it faced in the past.

How would you react if you were in Michael Smith's position? We are not all CEOs, but if you have any kind of leadership responsibility, a major challenge is the question of how to design your organization to encourage SuperLeadership as a natural and accepted form of leadership. Indeed, organizations find it difficult to obtain flexibility, initiative, and innovation from employees without providing widespread support for the practice of SuperLeadership and self-leadership.

In the previous two chapters we focused on the one-on-one relationship between a leader and a follower, as well as SuperLeadership through teams. For whole organizations, however, the best results derive from a total, integrated system that is deliberately intended to encourage, support, and reinforce self-leadership *throughout* the organization. Of course for the most part, this issue falls mainly within the responsibility of top management.

Nevertheless, as an individual manager or executive you can read this chapter from the viewpoint of your own responsibility—creating a self-leadership culture within your own departments. In this chapter we address the challenge of developing SuperLeadership throughout an organization. We focus mainly on the idea of encouraging SuperLeadership by influencing organizational culture. But first, let's briefly examine how SuperLeadership organizations can be created through organizational structure and through human resource systems.

CREATING SUPERLEADERSHIP THROUGH ORGANIZATIONAL STRUCTURES

The term "organizational structure" refers to the way tasks, roles, functions, and responsibilities are differentiated in an organization. As an example, in traditional organizations, differentiation is accomplished by separating the production function from the marketing function. In the past, these traditional and classic structures often produced an organization that was shaped like a tall pyramid and had a high degree of specialization in the different parts of the organization.

S *"To manage a large organization today is to manage a central paradox: how to develop strong leaders while decentralizing and de-layering the operations."*

—Steven Kerr[1]

Differentiation and specialization, of course, create a need for integration or coordination of the efforts of the specialized units. In the traditional organization this integration was typically accomplished through hierarchy, or a pyramidal structure where each level possessed increasing amounts of authority and responsibility. However, in today's information age we know that this traditional structure created the antithesis of what we now think of as an "empowered" organization. That is, task specialization disempowers employees, and the degree of self-leadership expected from disempowered employees is low.

The new information revolution is creating a sea of change in the way integration is taking place in organizations. Because of the speed and extent to which information can now be diffused through electronic networks, there is no longer a need for integration through hierarchy. In fact, new organizational structures have evolved over the past two decades that can speed the flow of information, diffuse decision-making authority, and empower even ordinary workers.

In addition, integration can be enhanced through the new Enterprise Resource Planning (ERP) systems, which cross traditional departmental lines and depend on the creative use of information technologies to get the right information to the person who needs it. Organizations structured around information flow can place the appropriate knowledge in the hands of the employee who needs the information for quick and flexible decision making. When information flows are designed on the basis of need rather than power, then followers will possess the knowledge and information that is truly necessary for empowerment. Enterprise Resource Planning systems like Oracle and SAP have the capacity to move information across departmental lines, bypassing the hierarchy and thus enhancing the potential for employee empowerment.

S *The lifeblood of today's organization structure is the rapid transformation of information, mainly through the Internet or Intranet.*

From the viewpoint of top management, new forms of organization structures can be used to enhance the possibilities of self-leadership throughout an organization. SuperLeaders want organizational structures that are less specialized and less differentiated. The first and most important of these structures is teams, especially empowered teams or self-managed teams. We devoted the previous chapter to this issue.

Overall, the most fundamental notion of developing self-leadership through organization structure is very consistent with the idea of the horizontal organization. Organizations moving toward the horizontal model are likely to use the following strategies:[2]

- Flatten the organization, removing unnecessary layers of management and supervision.

- Organize around key work processes (such as product development) rather than traditional functions.

- Place employees in work teams with the responsibility and authority largely to manage themselves.

- Reward employees on the basis of relevant work skills they possess and on team performance.

- Create plenty of occasions for employees to have regular contact with customers and suppliers.

- Provide employees with significant (even sensitive) information, and training to help them make effective decisions and perform their work well.

In summary, the traditional organization typically evolved into a taller pyramid structure, where hierarchy was used as the "glue" to hold the organization together. The fundamental purpose of that hierarchy was to provide channels for the exchange of information. For the organization of the 21st century, however, that hierarchy will be much less necessary because its integrative purpose has been replaced by information networks. Information will bind the parts of the organization together. Information will be the "glue" that holds organizations together.[3] Consider the following commentary from James Citrin and Thomas Neff, writing about leadership in the digital age:

The old way was a hierarchical structure in the shape of a pyramid. The structures of today require employees who are self-leaders to make them go. These structures can be described as flat, horizontal, decentralized, team-based, network-based, and alliance-based. The purpose, of course, is to develop that special flexibility and rapid response capability that will quickly seek out competitive advantage wherever it is to be found. According to Jack Welch, "the key to organizational success going forward will be to have the right person solving the most important business problem, no matter where they are located in the company hierarchically, organizationally, or geographically."[4]

CREATING SUPERLEADERSHIP THROUGH HUMAN RESOURCE SYSTEMS

The term "human resources," of course, refers to the people that work within an organization. The phrase "human resource strategy" is concerned with an organization's deliberate use of human resources to help it gain or maintain an edge against competitors in a marketplace.

Several generic areas of strategic decision choices are salient when managing human resources. Here are some of the more important decision choices that might be made:

- *Work flow:* choices between efficiency, high control, and explicit job descriptions versus innovation, flexibility, and broad job classes.

- *Staffing:* choices between informal hiring, internal recruitment, and line hiring versus formal hiring, external recruitment, and staff (HR department) hiring.

- *Performance appraisal:* choices between uniform appraisal procedures, control oriented, and supervisor input only versus flexible appraisals, developmental purpose, and multiple inputs.

- *Compensation:* choices between fixed pay, job-based pay, seniority pay, and centralized pay decisions versus variable pay, team-oriented pay, performance-based pay, and decentralized pay.

Compensation practices are particularly interesting when it comes to encouraging SuperLeadership and self-leadership throughout an organization. For example, does the pay system emphasize individual-based pay, where people are set into a competitive mode against each other, or does the system emphasize a team orientation where cooperation is the norm? Does the system tend to reward the accomplishment of narrow performance objectives, or is pay based at least in part on initiative and risk-taking?

An interesting example of the way compensation can be used to enhance self-leadership can be found at Saturn Corporation, the auto maker known for innovative organizational and marketing concepts that have broken ranks with the traditional practices of the auto industry. Saturn is well known as an organization that has attempted to place itself on the cutting edge in empowering all their employees. The pay plan at Saturn is based on four simple principles: (1) all employees are on salary, (2) there is a high degree of trust, (3) there are comparatively few job classifications, and (4) the system is founded in a pay-for-performance philosophy.

Another example of the way a human resource strategy can encourage self-leadership is through the innovative use of performance appraisal systems. For example, 360-degree appraisals solicit input from superior, peer, and subordinate levels. As a different example, several years ago Ford Motor Company started to use a performance appraisal system for executives that features a narrative feedback to each executive on "teamwork." The purpose, of course, is to encourage cooperative rather than competitive behavior in executive ranks.

Designing a culture that facilitates self-leadership can be addressed at different levels. The most ambitious approach within a single organization is to view the challenge from an overarching strategic human resource management perspective. Strategic vision is now considered a critical element in organizational success. More specifically, strategic design of entire human resource systems that foster effective self-leadership is indeed an ambitious and, it would seem, remarkably potent idea. The meshing of organizational structures, technologies, control systems, management styles, corporate cultures, training and development programs, and so forth—all of which bring out the best in people—is an exciting challenge.

S *The development of human resource management strategies designed to bring out the self-leadership capability of the work force is a critical organizational opportunity of the future.*

The notion of strategic management of human resources has achieved significant recognition within the last two decades. Many major corporations have now focused on this challenge and are currently addressing it with some vigor.

Overall, the point is clear: top-level strategic management need not and should not restrict itself to traditional concerns such as the economy, market opportunities, financial and product mixes, and the like. More specifically, successful SuperLeadership depends on the *strategic* creation of overarching human resource systems within which people can truly become self-leaders. Creating such environments will energize people and provide them with substitutes for bureaucratic control that can be flexibly adapted to varying situations. Yet the self-leadership culture provides stability and integration of effort, and an environment where human potential can be fully released. Within such systems, human initiative, creativity, determination, and inspiration can unfold.

CREATING AN ORGANIZATIONAL CULTURE OF SUPERLEADERSHIP

One concept that has received great attention over recent years is the notion of organizational culture. For years we have known that moving from one *national* culture to another brings many significant changes in a person's manner and style of living. More recently the powerful influences of distinct *organizational* cultures have been recognized by both organization scholars and executives. Organizations evolve their own unique pattern of values, folklore, rituals, traditions, style, and meaning, all of which significantly influence the behavior of organization members. An organization's culture could be termed a psychological environment—the mental or cognitive expectations that guide behavior.

One of the more interesting stories of creating a culture is the report of the experience of Commander D. Michael Abrashoff and the Navy destroyer USS Benfold.

"Yeah—all this SuperLeadership stuff is OK, but it won't work in the military!"

This is a comment that we have heard on several occasions. There seems to be a general stereotype that in a military environment only a Strongman type of leadership will work. We are not authorities on military leadership but we thought the story of the USS Benfold, a U.S. Navy destroyer, was an interesting counterexample to this stereotype.[5] The magazine *Fast Company* calls it "grassroots leadership," and we see it as self-leadership, as implemented by Super-Leader Commander D. Michael Abrashoff.

Abrashoff has set out to turn the traditional command-and-control system upside down, replacing it with a system that engages the minds and hearts of the ship's sailors. Even in the military, Abrashoff believes in empowerment. His leadership is guided by six principles:

▶ Don't just take command—communicate purpose.

▶ Leaders listen without prejudice.

▶ Practice discipline without formalism.

▶ The best captain hands out responsibility—not orders.

▶ Successful crews perform with devotion.

▶ True change is permanent.

Most of all, Abrashoff is guided by one principle: "I ask the people responsible—is there a better way to do things?" He frequently discovered there was a better way.

The results are impressive. The Benfold is one of the highest-performing ships in the U.S. Navy, racking up impressive scores in naval gunnery, readiness indicators, training, and redeployment turnaround. Perhaps the most impressive indicator is the Benfold's retention rate: Under Abrashoff's command, 100 percent of the Benfold's career sailors signed up for an additional tour.

Some experts have gone so far as to argue that strong, distinct corporate cultures may be the key to organizational survival and success.[6] The unique importance of culture is made evident by a company like Southwest Airlines, which encourages employees to develop diversity and humor in the ways they serve the public. The values and visions captured within the culture of an organization provide a unique kind of control mechanism—one that creates meaning, purpose, and commitment for employees.

The values and visions captured within the culture of an organization provide meaning, purpose, and commitment for employees.

Further, the various ingredients of corporate cultures can be important and powerful tools for weaving a fabric of high performance. Culture can be a crucial factor in facilitating successful implementation of corporate strategies. Indeed, an organizational culture will either support or hinder an organization's progress. When organizations make strategic shifts, their own unique culture is typically a great source of strength or weakness. Successful entry into a highly competitive market calling for aggressive risk-taking behavior, for example, may be difficult if there is a tradition in the firm of thoughtful, controlled, low-risk action. How ready was the AT&T culture, for example, to take on the demanding competition of a nonregulated environment? If new strategies violate employees' fundamental beliefs about their roles in the company, or about the traditions upon which the organization's culture is based, then failure is assured. Consider the following case, which was a high-profile rebellion against an overcontrolling culture:

A classic example of the demotivating influence of an overcontrolling culture is the Skylab 3 mission, launched on November 16, 1973. This story is particularly interesting because in its time, NASA was known as an organization on the cutting edge of management practice. After more than a month in space, highly trained and disciplined astronauts "turned off the radio and refused to talk with Houston Mission Control." This action has been characterized as the first strike in space.[7]

While the reasons leading to this action are complex, much of the cultural philosophy of ground controllers can be inferred from a quote from a prominent NASA official, described as a "tough, energetic flight director ... [who] was proud of the amount of control he could achieve."

"We send up about six feet of instructions to the astronauts' tele-printer every day—at least 42 separate instructions telling them where to point the solar telescope and which scientific instruments to use. We lay out the whole day for them, and they ... normally follow it to a T! What we've done is learned how to maximize what you can get out of a man in one day." Not surprisingly, this quote preceded the strike.

Obviously, this philosophy assumes a minimum of autonomy in space and further assumes that the maximum productivity can be gained by driving astronauts as if they were machines. This intolerance for self-leadership at NASA resulted in a strike in space. It has the faint echoes of Fredrick Taylor and the thousands of American managers of the past who believed that they could attain maximum productivity by controlling workers in a similar manner.

SuperLeadership at the top requires the creation of positive organizational cultures within which self-leadership can flourish. Such environments consist of a host of factors, some observable and concrete, others more subtle and symbolic. Overarching organizational values and goals that are part of a distinct corporate culture are just as important as the physical materials that are necessary for task performance. Training and development efforts that equip employees with both task-performance and self-leadership capabilities are important means of stimulating cultures based on leading others to lead themselves.

The SuperLeader's challenge is not limited to direct leadership; the SuperLeader must also foster an integrated world in which self-leadership can survive and grow, in which self-leadership becomes an exciting, motivating, and accepted way of life.

S *The SuperLeader's challenge is to foster an integrated world, where self-leadership becomes pervasive as an exciting, motivating, and accepted way of life.*

Culture weaves a delicate but powerful fabric that for many companies translates into effective achievement. An organizational culture can only be as strong as its weakest link, the single employee who meets the customer, so the self-leadership of each and every employee is of the utmost importance. Even one violation of an otherwise remarkable culture can stand out as a particularly ugly stain on what was once a handsome piece of cloth.

SuperLeadership and Culture

From a SuperLeadership view, culture becomes an important and legitimate means to exert leadership. Culture can be thought of as an evolution of acceptable responses that have worked in the past— patterns that were guided by the norms, values, and beliefs that existed during top managers' rise to power. But a true SuperLeader will develop an ability to recognize the culturally relevant needs of employees today—not yesterday—and devote significant effort to deliberately orchestrating an organizational culture for high performance and development of people.

S *Creating, articulating, and sustaining the organization's values thus becomes one of management's most important jobs.*[8]

The basic SuperLeadership elements that have been discussed in previous chapters are very relevant in meeting this challenge. The SuperLeader can model, encourage, provide guidance for, and reinforce the kinds of behaviors that will help create a positive cultural pattern. This cultural pattern should be centered on employee self-leadership: the SuperLeader will facilitate a culture founded upon the fundamental belief that effective self-leadership is critical for success. This culture recognizes the unique needs, strengths, and contributions of each individual, and facilitates the fullest development of each person. Most of all, a SuperLeader is a positive self-leadership model for others and helps employees to be models to each other. Furthermore, the SuperLeader will make it clear that such self-leadership behavior is not only allowed but expected. To accomplish this, the qualities of initiative, creativity, responsibility, and distinctiveness should be encouraged, reinforced, and viewed as the typical model of behavior. Consider the words of Evans and Wurster, who have recently written about how the Internet has "blown to bits" our conventional ways of doing business:

In [the new information] world, the traditional hierarchically defined roles of leadership become obsolete. But there remains [at least one] thing that leaders, and only leaders, can do.

[That is] creating a culture.

...The unique cultural values that a corporation builds ... are conscious and deliberate creations. They are established through incentives, through the selection of other leaders, and above all by *example*.

As ... structure and apparent stability prove ephemeral, as business boundaries ... melt into transience, the rich culture of the organization ... becomes a precious asset. *The* precious asset.

Culture—not factories, brands, business definitions, or patterns of ownership—defines the corporation. And that is uniquely the creation of *leadership*.[9]

Without any guidelines or integration of effort, a kind of anarchy would exist that would preclude common purpose and high performance. At the other extreme, rigid bureaucratic controls can stifle the initiative, creativity, and commitment required for excellence. Embedded in culture are the shared values, beliefs, and visions that provide the integrating mechanism that allows excitement and synergy at work to flourish. Many years ago, Peters and Waterman used the term, "loose-tight controls,"[10] which we believe entail control in a more subtle and indirect way through the norms of a Super-Leadership culture. In their leadership roles, SuperLeaders create a culture that facilitates self-leadership and allows the vast potential of the work force to flow.

Later, Robert Waterman expanded on this theme. He discussed the simultaneous provision of direction and the passing of power to the workforce. Managers at successful organizations that he calls "renewing companies" define the boundaries, and their subordinates figure out the best way to do the job within those boundaries. He calls this management style "an astonishing combination of direction and empowerment. The manager gives up tight control in order to gain more control over the end results."[11]

S *The SuperLeader will facilitate a culture that is founded upon the fundamental belief that effective self-leadership is critical for success.*

Top-management SuperLeaders are concerned with developing a self-leadership culture throughout the organization. At lower levels, the challenge for aspiring SuperLeaders is to develop subcultures within their own areas that stimulate the unique self-leadership strengths of each person. The evolving culture becomes an integrated environment within which diversity, self-leadership, and future excellence are nourished. Again, the SuperLeader musters the strength of ten and more—a strength that is founded on the unique multiple abilities of others rather than on the limited qualities of one person who happens to be called the leader. This challenge is indeed difficult, especially for very large, complex organizations. Nevertheless, faced with a rapidly changing global economy, many U.S. corporations have undertaken a substantial revitalization of their organizational culture.

CULTURE AND SUPERLEADERSHIP: MORE THAN THE CEO

Obviously, strategic efforts toward self-leadership organizations are important. But, an employee might object, "Hey, I'm not a CEO. I can't change the total culture of my organization." Indeed, the primary target of this book is the individual executive or aspiring executive. While these individuals are sometimes in a position to influence the overall organizational strategic process, the most important target involves their influence on the subcultures within which their own immediate followers perform. Most executives are faced with the challenge of managing only a part within a total organization, but this influence is nevertheless very important.

The SuperLeader will know how to take advantage of this opportunity to create a backdrop for performance that brings out the best in subordinates. Through this effort, the organization's culture as a whole moves in the direction of an integrated self-leadership system.

An organization's personality and character are largely manifestations of each of the subcultures that executives and managers spawn within their own areas of responsibility.

In this chapter we have provided some ideas about how Super-Leaders can create integrated systems that are fertile for self-leadership. Sometimes, as we read our own writing, the words make this task seem easy. But it's not. The key task, from an overall organizational viewpoint, is to move toward self-leadership and all its benefits without (as one colleague put it) "going off in 26 directions at once." Achieving this objective is challenging, and it begins and ends with managers moving toward self-leadership within their own spheres of influence.

For a SuperLeader to achieve long-term, lasting success in stimulating self-leadership in others, significant attention should be given to establishing and maintaining a constructive overall system of self-leadership. The character and personality of larger organizational cultures are born from the aggregate of the many smaller cultures that are spawned throughout the firm. Positive subcultures emphasizing the self-leadership of every person can generate a true holistic culture where SuperLeaders lead others to lead themselves.

(More) Dennis Bakke
of AES Corporation

Ken A. Smith

We now return to Dennis Bakke and AES Corporation. Our earlier profile showed that Bakke embraces values that reflect SuperLeadership and that he has been effective at modeling and fostering self-leadership in a very personal way. But what happens when a company grows? Even with annual plant visits and an "open door" policy, the corporate leader cannot have a personal relationship with every employee. So how does a SuperLeader foster self-leadership beyond his or her immediate sphere of influence? At AES it happens because of choices that have been made about organizational processes and structures.

REINFORCING SELF-LEADERSHIP
THROUGHOUT THE ORGANIZATION

Bakke reinforces self-leadership with regard to business operations by providing for the free flow of information throughout the company—so that people making decisions have ready access to necessary information. One structural unit that supports the free flow of information is AES's strategy group. Rather than engage in traditional strategic planning, this group provides people throughout the company with information on environmental changes, technological developments, and the like. As much strategic information as possible is shared. Bakke notes, "We have very few secrets at AES. Even the details of potential acquisition decisions are shared."[1] Why? Because there is lots of corporate experience, and those making decisions on the front lines should benefit from that experience. Thus, financial and market information is also widely distributed. And employees have responded in kind, volunteering information that will benefit others. For example when Flora Zhou was bidding on a deal in Vietnam, she posted a request for relevant information via the company's e-mail system. Sarah Slusser, a manager in Central America who had experience on a venture with similar characteristics, provided valuable insight into how the project should be pursued.

Self-leadership relative to AES's core values is reinforced through an extensive values survey that is completed annually by every person who works in a plant that is at least 50 percent owned by AES. Bakke reads every one of the 10,000 surveys, looking for indications of how the company is doing on its values. As Bakke said, "A few years ago I noticed that a lot of people from the same plant wrote in their surveys, 'Why do we have to buy plants abroad? We should just stay in the United States and provide jobs to Americans.' From that, I could tell that the plant manager and team leaders there were not doing a good job of making our mission to meet needs *in the world* understood. And those attitudes also called into question whether people were adhering to the principles of fairness and social responsibility."[2] In addition to the general values survey, each manager is rated annually on "values performance"—that is, how he or she performs in relation to the four shared values. According to Bakke, "We rate each other, fifty-fifty, on the basis of technical performance and values performance." When it is determined that a manager has compromised the company's values, his or her compensation can be affected in such ways as losing part or all of any performance bonus.

 Performance evaluation is a supportive process, focused on balancing business performance and value performance.

More broadly, Bakke encourages all AES employees to challenge any and all others on how strategic and operating decisions reflect the core values. This fosters an air of mutual accountability, and serves as a constant reminder that all are members of the same team. "But," says Bakke, "*supportive* doesn't mean glossing over someone's problems. Evaluation meetings can be very intense. We push one another. We want to help one another be the best we can be in stewarding resources to meet the world's need for electricity."[3]

CONSTRUCTIVE REPRIMAND, WITH AN EMPHASIS ON SELF-LEADERSHIP

When mistakes occur, and they do, Bakke and his top management are quick to address them directly—and to own up to their own responsibility. For example in 1992, company insiders discovered—and reported—that technicians at the Shady Point, Oklahoma, plant had falsified results of water-quality tests sent to the Environmental Protection Agency. Although the plant did not actually release pollutants into the river, the news drove AES stock down from $26.50 to $16.50 in one day and the company was forced to pay a $125,000 fine. Those involved received reprimands and reductions in pay. Some were reassigned. However, in keeping with AES's commitment to its people, none was fired. Rather, each was given the opportunity to take responsibility, recover from the event, and do better in the future. Although several did eventually leave the company, they did so voluntarily. Those who remained learned from the experience and have pursued successful careers since.

As an aside, it should be noted that Bakke is quite ready to fire someone when it is warranted. In an interview with *Business Week*, Bakke noted, "One of the least socially responsible things in the world is to have one extra person working when they're not needed. In other words, an unproductive person. When they're added to the rest of the group, it makes the whole group unproductive. In either case it's a travesty to the society to keep that person in an unproductive role. The compassion comes with how you do [the firing] and what responsibility you take for that transition. As much as I feel strongly about letting people go, in 99 percent of the cases they're doing it voluntarily. We're paying them significant amounts of money and letting them choose whether they want to stay or want to go. So we're paying enormous amounts of money in order to soften this transition from unproductive activity to productive activity."[4]

The events at Shady Point drove Bakke and top management to the conclusion that they had failed in this instance to fully communicate the importance of the company's values. So seriously did they take the breach that in addition to reprimanding those involved, top management also took a pay cut and gave up their own bonuses for the year. In essence, this became a type of self-reprimand. The event also proved to be a watershed for AES's system of values. A debate erupted between those who believed the company needed to tighten controls and those committed to empowering employees. "For me it was a major crisis," said Bakke, who "was prepared to leave before tearing apart the company's management model. It took time to work out. For a year and a half after the incident, the Shady Point plant operated with a self-imposed layer of supervision and a dedicated environmental staff. But eventually, employees chose to revert to the company's standard [self-management] approach."[5]

BUILDING A CULTURE THAT FOSTERS SELF-LEADERSHIP

Bakke and the management team at AES have sought to give legs to self-leadership by building a culture that fosters creativity—often at the expense of efficiency. Bakke believes that an over-emphasis on efficiency hurts people and organizations. Says Bakke, "Ours is a very inefficient organization. I'll tell you that right now. We are very inefficient. But we're pretty effective, I think." Pushed for a definition of inefficiency, Bakke explains, "Well, we always try to learn things new again. I purposely have people reinventing the wheel."

An example is the way AES develops new projects: "There's a team—everything is organized around a team—that's doing development of a project," says Bakke. "We have thousands of regulations and all kinds of environmental impact things that you have to do. And you have people around the community who are hostile and don't want us to be there. And we have huge amounts of technical work that has to be done to get the plant ready: find out how it's going to be engineered, what it's going to look like, and so forth. And we have electric contracts to sign and make sure of, and we have financing to do for a $400 million facility. And lots of contracts for fuel. All this stuff going on, okay? We've done it all before....What do we do? Reassign tasks. The team member that did one thing on a previous project will do something else on the current project. Last time they did financing, this time they're doing air permits. And the team will change, so there's no repository of all the data that says how you do it, and none of us will say, 'OK, here's what we did last time' unless the guy comes to us and says, 'What did you do in this situation?' There's no forcing them to follow any prescribed set that says 'You have to do this and this and this and here's how you get this done. Here's how you do this. This is what we did last time.' Now they do ask and they get a lot of information, but the decision is theirs. . . . Their objective is to get the plant built. They don't need to be told to follow certain directions, to be told, 'Here's the rule book,' because there isn't any rule book. If there was we got rid of it. We want them to recreate and change it, because the world's different every time they go out there. We want a learning organization; we're constantly forcing people to redo things."

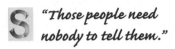

S *"Those people need nobody to tell them."*

According to Bakke, the trade-off against efficiency is worth it because of the sense of control and total responsibility that people feel when they really own their decisions. It changes people forever. They become better business people, better employees, and better team members, whose ability to lead themselves benefits the company as a whole.

DEVELOPING SELF-MANAGING TEAMS

Consistent with a learning organization, AES evokes psychological ownership through the use of teams throughout the company, not just for business development. This has not always been the case; AES's first projects were organized as traditional functional bureaucracies. But not for long.

"Our plants were running wonderfully," Bakke recalls, "when we said 'This isn't really consistent with our values and the way we want people to operate and relate to each other. We need to make huge changes in the way we do operations if we're going to be consistent with our values.' We did this massive change that came to be known as Operation Honeycomb. We changed how our plants are organized and how people relate to each other. . . . We didn't want arbitrary rules, detailed procedures manuals and handbooks, punch clocks, etc. We wanted a 'learning organization,' where people close to the action were constantly creating and recreating and where these people were making the decisions—strategy, financial, and capital allocations. For example, I went down and asked, 'What if you didn't have shift supervisors? What if you didn't have this manual that tells you everything to do?' Two months later, they totally revolutionized the place."

S *"It's based on the premise that people will take responsibility and can be trusted."*

"We outlined several elementary principles to be used in a Honeycomb structure. Cut the number of supervisor levels to improve communication, and get out of people's way. And then one of the plant people came up with 'Why don't we just divide up into teams?' The next thing I knew, the plant manager called me and said, 'We got this all done. We've implemented it.' They said, 'We're going to call this stuff "Honeycomb"'—and they had worked out all this symbolism regarding beehives and how all the bees were working together."

Today, all of AES's plants are organized around some form of self-managing teams. Since the process of change essentially is implemented bottom-up (although mandated top-down), the specific forms, labels, and language vary considerably from plant to plant; there is no cookie-cutter approach. Further, the path leading to self-management has been quite different among the plants. Some were "changeovers" of existing nonunion plants; one was a changeover of a union plant; others have had a team structure from the beginning.

This variety of implementation and form has given AES a tremendous diversity of experience as they have adapted to the specific conditions unique to each plant. Nevertheless, the conversion to "honeycomb" teams has always been inspired and guided by the core values of the organization, and always features a bottom-up process that displays great confidence that the employees have a special capability to work out the details of implementation that will suit them best. "Most important," says Bakke, "is that Honeycomb provides an environment where the 'fun' value can best work itself out for each AES person."

SUPERLEADERSHIP: WHO MAKES DECISIONS?

Bakke has been so successful at leading others to lead themselves that he has given up almost all decisions. He told *Harvard Business Review*, "This year I made two decisions, which was one more than I made last year. I made the decision about how many regional groups we would have and who would lead them. Those were big decisions, so I took six months to make them.

I really played them out because if you only make two decisions a year, you want to play them for all they are worth. As for the rest of the decisions (strategic, planning, capital allocation, and so on) that needed to be made for AES—well, they were made by the people out there who are right on top of the problems or issues or opportunities."[6]

So what does Bakke do as SuperLeader? He identifies five roles. "My dream would be that our leaders would be first and foremost the keepers of, the interpreters of, the teachers of our principles and values. That's my first role. My second role is to be chief adviser. My third role: After people make decisions, we start holding everybody accountable. If they're not being held accountable by their colleagues, then the leader steps in and has to be chief accountability officer. The fourth role is chief celebrator, cheerleader. Then, in some cases it's not clear who should make a decision. There are some decisions where it's not obvious, for example, when there are conflicts between geographic areas. So my fifth role is to pick the person who will in fact make the ultimate decision. That goes back to the one decision I make a year. I get to divide up the world. A very powerful job. I get to reassign things in terms of our groups."[7]

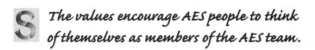

The values encourage AES people to think of themselves as members of the AES team.

Bakke's emphasis on AES's shared values has contributed to the team spirit that pervades the company. Integrity stresses the need for individuals to fulfill commitments—their own and those made by the company. Fairness generates sensitivity to the positions and perspectives of others, both in and outside the company. Fun, as defined at AES, results from using one's abilities to contribute to the effort of the whole. Social responsibility stresses being aware of and serving the needs of others. Together these values build an outward-looking orientation in the minds of AES personnel, and foster a desire to take personal responsibility to work with and for the benefit of the team. Bakke provides this powerful story:

"Let me give you one example of what happened, the kind of thing I think we've had example after example of. We had a guy who, after this Honeycomb process, went Saturday shopping with his wife at one of the discount stores.

He was waiting around, waiting for her to get done, and he noticed that they had fans on sale. He looked at the fans, and he realized that they were almost the same kind of fans that we were using at the plant in the process of making gypsum at the back end of our plant. We use a lot of them; they end up wearing out because there's a pretty dirty atmosphere, and so they burn out real fast. He saw that they were selling them for something like $24 apiece, and he remembered that we were spending $75 from the original manufacturer who supplied them at first, and we kept going back to the same guy, at $75. Once or twice a month we were paying to get new fans. So he immediately took his credit card and bought the entire stock in the store, period. Just bought it."

"Now that is the kind of action we're talking about. This is a nonsupervisor, just a regular guy in the plant. What had to be the situation for him? First of all, he had to understand what the technology was, that it was the same kind. He was aware that this was the same kind of fan, or very similar to it, and it would do the same thing in the plant. Second, he had to know all the cost numbers. Third, he had to know that he had authority to do it—that it was safe. And if he was wrong, it would be okay. Because if he really feared for his job in doing this, or that he would have to pay for these hundreds of dollars of fans he had just bought, for a normal guy . . . he knew he would be backed up on it."

Such willingness to take individual responsibility, such self-leadership, demonstrates the effectiveness of SuperLeadership. Bakke and AES constantly encourage this kind of behavior. Says Bakke, "We're trying to publicize it and be happy to have more people do it, every day. That kind of wraps it up."

Part IV

SuperLeadership
in the 21st Century

A great (leader) is someone who says,
You come to work with me, and I'll help you be as successful as possible;
I'll help you grow;
I'll help you make sure you're in the right role;
I'll provide the relationship for you to understand and know yourself.
And I want you to be more successful than me.
—Marcus Bullingham and Curt Coffman[1]

Leadership:
A Hero or Hero-Maker?

"**W**ow!
We're in charge!"

These were the thoughts running through the minds of Drew Morris and Shervin Pishevar as they awaited their flight from Baltimore to San Francisco. Shervin and Drew are the 26-year-old cofounders of WebOS, Inc., an Internet startup firm focusing on developing an operating system that would run not on computers, but through the Internet.[1]

Shervin, first-generation son of Iranian immigrants and graduate of the University of California at Berkeley, thinks about the future as he waits. He is clearly a gifted individual and was an honor student earning high marks. Drew Morris, the son of a successful entrepreneur, received an undergraduate business degree from Emory and has an extensive technical background. Since finishing school a couple years ago, both have turned down many jobs offering high salaries so they could pursue their dream of being entrepreneurs.

Their grand vision is to provide a viable alternative to traditional operating systems such as Windows and Macintosh by creating a Web-based operating system that would allow users to access and use their files on any Internet-connected PC, handheld device, or Web-enabled cell phone. Finally, after developing several business plans, and a lot of hard work, Shervin and Drew were able to obtain substantial venture capital for their startup. With the prospective breakup of Microsoft, they see new opportunities for their company. They have even opened a San Francisco office, and are now looking for a third round of venture capital. Now on the second anniversary of the start-up, Shervin and Drew ponder their future and the future of WebOS.

"What kind of a company do we want to build?" they ask each other. "I know it won't be easy, but we both want the company to be guided by a certain philosophy and values. What should they be?"

Shervin and Drew face an imposing leadership challenge. How would you advise them? What would you do if you were in their position? Vast technological changes have drastically altered the world of organizations. And these changes have had pervasive effects on the kind of leadership demanded in this new information- and knowledge-based world. How would you meet the kind of challenges faced by these two young entrepreneurs? What are your views on the best way to lead the knowledge workers of the 21st century?

Throughout this book we have proposed an approach to leadership that we have described as the *New SuperLeadership*. We have provided many examples that illustrate how this might unfold in practice. In this final chapter we share some of our concluding thoughts about how leaders can change themselves. Do you want to be a hero or a hero-maker?

SuperLeadership: A Way to Meet the Challenge of Leading in the 21st Century

As we move further into the new century and the new millennium, we believe this is a great time to be in business. With the aid of advanced technology, employee productivity and product quality have risen steadily and American business has reemerged as a world leader. Opportunities for achieving great things and for experiencing fulfillment in work and life have never been greater. Medical advances and increased standards of living have enabled people to enjoy longer and healthier lives. And scientific advances have provided many impressive technologies, such as automated factories, robotics, palm computers, biotechnology, and advanced information systems, that only a few decades ago would have seemed impossible. If we take stock of the positive opportunities that exist for corporations and their employees, it's difficult to be blind to all of the potential.

 It's not what you know anymore, but knowing how to learn that's important.

But so too, the challenges are great. It's highly unlikely that people can reasonably expect to learn everything they'll need to be successful in their careers during "school years." How would you advise them? What would you do if you were in their position? Life-long learning is no longer a luxury; it's now a requirement for survival. Most people cannot possess all the knowledge required to perform their work. If we truly aspire to high performance, we need to be continually learning and benefiting from the knowledge of others.

Most of all, the 21st century has brought us many challenges and many opportunities for leadership. Leadership can no longer be restricted to a select few who are given special power and authority. Each of us must be involved in order to fully use the knowledge and information that form the bedrock of work life in the high-tech new world of the third millennium. Self-leadership is the key to enhancing the learning that is necessary to enable us to meet the challenges of this information-rich and knowledge-based era. And SuperLeadership provides the tools for leaders to be able to create this self-leadership in others. A good illustration of many of these features is provided by the high-performance practices of Nokia.

Nokia has now passed Motorola to become the leading seller of mobile phones.[2] By most measures of financial performance, Nokia has been an amazing success—in 1999 Nokia led market share with 27 percent and the highest European stock market value, and was named by *Business Week* as the number one information technology company in the world.[3] Yet, this technology-leading company is a 135-year-old corporation located in the small northern country of Finland. Despite its age and tradition, Nokia seems to be able to innovate again and again with products that lead the market.

Fortune magazine describes Nokia as perhaps the "least hierarchical big company in the world." According to *Fortune*, much of the credit for the remarkable performance of Nokia lies in the philosophy of empowerment fostered and encouraged by their CEO, Jorma Ollila. The Nokia way of doing things is especially team-oriented, starting at the top. Almost every decision of importance is vested in some type of team. According to Matti Alahuhta, head of mobile phones, "The objective is to always have decisions made by the people who have the best knowledge."[4]

To outsiders, this form of organization sometimes seems to be totally confused—sort of a "who's in charge?" type of syndrome. Yet, to insiders who have become accustomed to the Nokia culture, the process seems to be creative and effective. "People who join Nokia spend a few months trying to figure it out," according to Kevin Knowles, an American manager at Nokia's U.S. headquarters. "You really have to figure out a network of people to get things done." Tony Mitchell, a Nokia manager located in Texas, describes the Nokia culture as a system of shared values. "[It's] unique to Nokia—the freedom a group is allowed to take. There are certain shared systems we keep as standard, but you're allowed to be creative."

Nokia has a unique method of bottom-up strategic planning. Nokia people start each year with gatherings all over the world. Their purpose is to creatively reexamine Nokia's priorities. The result of their deliberations is communicated upward to the top management team, who use this information to reevaluate the strategic vision for the company. The cycle is complete when this vision is diffused back throughout the company through management presentations.

Most of all, CEO Ollila provides a model of SuperLeadership in the way he organizes the top management team. The five top executives have worked together for a significant period. Many see the five as an inseparable unit.

But the glue that holds the team together seems to be Ollila, who has a unique way of running Nokia—that is, he lets other people run it. The results are obvious—a world-class company that leads in creativity, entrepreneurship, and personal responsibility. Ollila has his own unique method for promoting self-leadership.

SuperLeadership is radically unlike the classic stereotypes of strong leadership. The profiles we have presented provide only glimpses of the many ways that the SuperLeadership approach has been pursued by current and past leaders in many different facets of society. And SuperLeadership is a process that can be *learned*, that is not restricted to a few "special" individuals who are born to be great. Granted, some seem to have more to learn than others. But in the end, all of us typically want to move toward a new, more effective leadership.

First, SuperLeaders master self-leadership for themselves. Then they encourage and model it for others. They facilitate employee self-set-goals and reward effective self-leadership when it does occur. Overall, they create and nurture systems that allow teamwork and a holistic self-leadership culture to flourish. SuperLeadership unleashes increased employee performance and innovation that is rooted in enhanced commitment, motivation, and employee creativity.

LEADERSHIP.COM

One point is clear: the rapidly changing technology of the 21st century is creating structures that call for new forms of leadership. The most remarkable change is the way information and communication can be conveyed. The information revolution is well under-way, but we are only beginning to emerge into the "wireless" phase of that revolution. All of us now have the option of being "connected" no matter where we are and no matter when it is.

The availability of information creates special opportunities for self-leadership. The Internet, for example, has amply demonstrated how information can create prospects for self-organizing systems. The Linux computer operating system is an example of how information has created a self-sustaining system. Linux is an ongoing collaboration of thousands of software writers who make individual bottom-up contributions to evolve the Linux system. The availability of open information makes this sort of system feasible. While Linux is a between-organizations system, SuperLeaders can create within-organization self-organizing systems through the creative use of information networks. The need for traditional hierarchy is dead. Information makes true self-leadership possible.

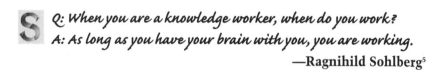

Q: When you are a knowledge worker, when do you work?
A: As long as you have your brain with you, you are working.
—Ragnihild Sohlberg[5]

What does this amazing change in technology mean in terms of leadership? On the one hand, one could imagine a world where Strongman leadership becomes feasible in the extreme. We know, for example, that privacy is gone and that finely grained surveillance can be implemented. If desired, the technology exists for leaders to watch and control their followers in almost every waking moment.

Yet an opposite type of scenario is also feasible and, we believe, more likely. That is, people are more likely to be operating on their own. We see trends such as "distributed" work, where people are not located together—working at home, virtual teams. In essence the relationship between a leader and followers is likely to be less dependent on physical presence.

In these cases, the functions that used to be served by organizational hierarchy can be replaced by information networks and empowered employees. Coordination, communication, and access to information can be available to all, and—providing they have the education, skill, training, and capability—authority can also be distributed. That is, we believe the information revolution will fuel the trend to an empowered organization where authority is widely distributed to all parts and all levels.

There are several advantages to fostering an empowered organization:

- Technology is moving fast—it's likely that your followers know more about technological advances than you do.

- You can't always be there to watch your followers.

- Followers can move faster and more effectively if they talk to each other without having to "clear" things through you.

- Speed of response is improved—empowered followers can respond to customers or changes without waiting for you.

- Flexibility is improved.

- Creativity is improved—people may do it in a different way.

Of course, there are some concomitant disadvantages:

- If there is one "best" way of doing it, there are likely to be more deviations.

- It may, at times, just seem like chaos.

- It can give one the feeling that everything is out of control.

SuperLeadership is ideally suited for the information revolution. Followers expect SuperLeadership; indeed, they demand it. Information becomes a type of "substitute" for traditional leadership. With information and networking, traditional leadership as represented by the organizational hierarchy is not required. The new SuperLeadership employs a form of active leadership that concentrates on developing the self-leadership capabilities of followers so that they can truly take advantage of the information revolution.

BEYOND WINDOW DRESSING:
REAL SELF-LEADERSHIP ON THE FRONT LINES

True SuperLeaders clearly communicate that initiative and self-direction are not only wanted but expected. Getting this message out is a key component of the SuperLeader's job. Unfortunately, what on the surface looks like an effort to encourage self-leadership can sometimes turn out to be mere window dressing unless it is supported by a sincere commitment to advanced levels of empowerment throughout the organization. The following example illustrates this risk.

A few years ago, one of the major international hotel chains with headquarters in the U.S. developed a new policy to guide decision making throughout their far-flung worldwide operations. According to this new policy, the intention was to push actual decisions to the lowest level possible. In theory this meant that the critical decisions of when and where to open a new property should be made within the appropriate geographical region rather than U.S. headquarters. The major purpose of this well-intentioned change was to provide more timely decisions that were not retarded by communication delays up and down the vertical hierarchy.

The essential question, however, is whether self-leadership becomes a matter of rhetoric or a matter of practice. While the following incident is entirely a figment of our own imagination, it is based on some actual knowledge of the past culture of this giant international corporation. We could imagine the following conversation taking place:

Jonathan gazed out over the magnificent view of the harbor from his office high in the skyscraper located on Hong Kong Island. Despite seeing the view for almost five years, he still was occasionally amazed at the busy traffic between the island and the Kowloon section on the other side. Jonathan was vice president of Far East operations for the corporation. One of his responsibilities was to oversee the development of new properties in Asia, especially the rapidly developing market for Western-style hotels in the People's Republic of China.

He turned to Francine Chung, the director of development for Far East properties. "Look at this new policy statement," he said. "According to this, decision making is to be pushed out into the geographical regions. Theoretically, we have full authority to make the new development decisions for Asia."

"Great!" replied Francine. "We should be able to move a little faster. We have had considerable trouble getting approvals from headquarters for our plans. And our competition is clearly moving fast."

"In fact," she continued, "why don't we start the new contracts for the property near the new airport in Shanghai. We definitely know we want it and if we don't move, our competitor will beat us in."

"Well," mused Jonathan, "let's not get out ahead of ourselves. I've learned one thing about this company over the years, sometimes the hard way. It's one thing to say I have the authority—it's another thing when it comes to really exercising that authority."

"I'm not sure what you mean," said Francine.

"It works like this. Theoretically, I may have the authority for a certain decision. But in the past I've learned that if I go ahead and make that decision and then—after the fact—my boss doesn't like it, I find my rear end in deep trouble."

"In fact," he continued, "over the years I've learned to do it this way—that is, don't actually make the decision until it's been cleared by my boss. Of course what this really means is that I'm not really making the decision."

"Yeah," said Francine, with a bit of sarcasm, "but your boss does the same thing. And the reality is that no decision really gets made except at headquarters—and that's why it takes so long!"

"Now you've got it," said Jonathan. "I know you want to move on Shanghai but first we need to make sure that we have the go-ahead from headquarters."

"The more things change, the more things stay the same," replied Francine.

The main point to this story should be clear—one can theoretically promote self-leadership through policy pronouncements, but it's the behavior itself that really makes the difference. In the case of this hotel giant, decisions will not actually be decentralized until things move beyond carefully selected language in policy statements, to the point that "headquarters" says, "This is your decision—make it!"

 "To compete . . . companies must tend to their knowledge workers as a farmer tends to his land."

—**Charles Fishman**[6]

SuperLeadership is not just rhetoric, it is action oriented. Super-Leadership is only "super" if the strength, knowledge, and creativity of the knowledge workers of the information age are unleashed. Self-leadership becomes the norm instead of the exception. The Super-Leader's "strength of ten and more" is rooted in the self-leadership of others. This means "clearing things with bosses" and "rear protecting" is exchanged for empowerment, speed, and commitment. No more waiting for the boss to make a decision . . . everyone's a leader!

Moreover, SuperLeadership is sustainable. Consider the case of the Consolidated Diesel Co. facility at Whitakers, N.C., a joint venture between Cummins Engine and J.I. Case Corp.:

Formed in 1980 as a joint venture between Cummins Engine Co. and J.I. Case Corp., Consolidated Diesel's plant represents an ongoing social experiment that poses a deceptively simple question: Will granting people an extraordinary level of responsibility allow them to achieve an extraordinary level of performance?

After 19 years, the same answer keeps coming back: Yes ![7]

SuperLeadership at Its Essence

So what is the essential message of *The New SuperLeadership*? If we forget everything else, what must we remember? Here is our summary, or what we call:

The SuperLeadership Survival Guide

What is Leadership?

▸ Leadership is influence, especially influence of the behavior and thoughts of others. For people in organizations, leadership especially means influencing their performance.

▸ Leadership can be brought to bear in many ways. Among the most prominent types of leadership are these three: Strongman (authoritarian), Transactor (rewarding), and Visionary Hero (inspiring).

▸ Each of these types of leadership has unique advantages and disadvantages. A real leader might use all types at different times.

What is Self-Leadership and why is it so important?

▸ The main source of influence comes from within. We call this self-leadership—the influence that we direct toward ourselves to organize and motivate our own behavior, thoughts, and performance.

▸ Self-leadership is not something we are born with. Each of us can learn to be a better self-leader.

▸ Self-leadership can be implemented by influencing one's own: (1) behavior and actions, (2) natural rewards, and (3) mind and thoughts (see the specific self-leadership strategies of chapters 4, 5, and 6).

---

*What is SuperLeadership and what
does it have to do with self-leadership?*

▶ Leaders can influence the self-leadership of others. That is,
they can stimulate followers to be self-leaders. We call
this SuperLeadership—leading others to lead themselves.
It's a form of empowerment.

▶ SuperLeadership involves leading others to influence their
own behavior and performance. The primary aim of
SuperLeadership is the development, mentoring, and
unleashing of the capability of followers. It is an *active*
form of leadership.

▶ A SuperLeader empowers, coaches, teaches, rewards, and
arranges circumstances to enable followers to lead themselves and enhance their own performance.

▶ SuperLeadership can be expressed at three levels: toward
the individual, the team, and the organizational culture.

*How can SuperLeadership be put into practice
to bring out self-leadership in others?*

▶ SuperLeaders promote self-leadership by listening more
and talking less; asking more questions and giving fewer
answers; encouraging more learning and using less punishment; encouraging more teamwork and discouraging
infighting; fostering more initiative and creativity and less
conformity; and so forth.

▶ SuperLeaders choose their behavior with a persistent
intention to create independence and interdependence and
to avoid creating dependence.

> ◆ SuperLeaders serve as living models of dynamic self-leadership and reinforce others to take responsibility and to lead themselves.
>
> ◆ SuperLeaders gain the strength of many (the strength to be SuperLeaders) by striving to turn so-called followers into self-leaders who bring their full talents, experience, and capability to their work.

The bottom line is that none of us can become "super" as a leader on our own. Leaders unleash and gain the strength of many by leading others to lead themselves. In the process they experience a metamorphosis—they become SuperLeaders.

SEARCHING: NOT FOR HEROIC LEADERS BUT FOR HERO-MAKERS

SuperLeadership offers the most viable approach for establishing exceptional self-leaders in the workplace in this modern age. In today's world, compliance from followers is not enough. Leading others to lead themselves is the key to tapping the intelligence, the spirit, the creativity, the commitment, and most of all the tremendous, unique potential of each person.

Our perspective is straightforward. Any aspiring SuperLeader can choose no better strategy than nurturing and harvesting the vast capabilities of those who surround them. SuperLeadership means tapping into a power of employee capability that transcends the imagination. This book has been written for those who wish to become SuperLeaders by discovering how to lead others to lead themselves.

It is time to transcend the notion of leaders as heroes and to focus instead on leaders as hero-makers. Is the spotlight on the leader, or on the follower? If you want to be a great leader of others, first learn to lead yourself. Then encourage and help others to do the same, and reward them when they break the bonds of dependency. All the while, you will be creating a culture of exceptional achievement based on exceptional self-leaders. That's the simple message of this book. True SuperLeadership is *not* about attracting the admiration of others with great charisma and vision. That approach only increases the attention on the leader at the expense of all the others. Instead, the object is to develop so-called followers into dynamic self-leaders that are inspired by their own potential and effectiveness.

 It is time to transcend the notion of leaders as heroes and to focus instead on leaders as hero-makers.

In fact, so-called charismatic or transformational leaders too often turn out to be a smoothed-out version of the dictatorial, autocratic leaders of past generations—leaders who bend the will of others to their own, not by threat or fear but by capitalizing on an artificial sense of the leader's greatness or superiority. Visionary, charismatic leaders who possess a broad view of the organization and its environment can be very important, especially in the short term during a crisis or major organizational change, and particularly in cases of disarray, where the organizational culture has lost its direction and sense of competence. Iacocca at Chrysler and Jobs at Apple did wonders as their organizations teetered on the brink of collapse. But in the long run, overemphasizing visionary or charismatic leadership can foster a dependence that can actually weaken the system.

Is the spotlight on the leader, or on the achievements of others?

Visionary leadership based on charisma can create a system that is not able to function in the absence of the leader, a system that collapses like a house of cards when the leader moves on. With charismatic leadership, the power and vision are vested in the leader, so the followers become as empty vessels. But with Super-Leadership, the power and the vision rest in the followers. The so-called followers stand as strong pillars of self-leadership that support the overall system for the long haul.

 We are talking about a new breed of leader, a SuperLeader. . . .
To find them simply look at their followers.
SuperLeaders have SuperFollowers.

In the end, we are talking about a new breed of leader, a Super-Leader, one that turns leadership inside out, upside down, and literally on its ear. To discover this new breed of leader, a person must simply look—*not* at the leader, but at the followers. SuperLeaders have SuperFollowers who are dynamic self-leaders. SuperLeaders are not heroes, they are hero-makers. And these ideas are not really new. They are based on the wisdom of the ages. Perhaps they were most effectively expressed in a poem by Lao Tzu, a sixth-century B.C. Chinese philosopher. We quoted these words at the beginning. So, as a fitting close to our book, we end by again offering these words as a gift to you, the SuperLeaders of tomorrow.

A leader is best

When people barely know he exists,

Not so good when people obey and acclaim him,

Worse when they despise him.

But of a good leader, who talks little,

When his work is done, his aim fulfilled,

They will say:

We did it ourselves.

—Lao Tzu

Notes

Chapter 1: Leadership in the 21st Century

1. Quoted by James M. Citrina and Thomas J. Neff, "Digital Leadership," *Strategy & Business Journal*, 18 (First Quarter, 2000), p. 45.
2. Michael Dertouzos, *What Will Be: How the New World of Information Will Change Our Lives* (San Francisco: Harper Collins, Harper Edge, 1997).
3. These predictions are a direct quote from: "The Mobile Century: Work Is What We Do, Not Where We Do It," *Business Week* (June 19, 2000), p. 144.
4. This table was inspired and adapted from *Visions of the Future*: Flowchart Report from the Corporate Leadership Council, Washington, D.C., and Chapter 18, *Company of Heroes*, by Henry P. Sims, Jr., and Charles C. Manz (Wiley, 1996).
5. Robert E. Kelley, *The Gold-Collar Worker* (New York: Addison-Wesley, 1985).
6. S. Kerr, "GE's Collective Genius," *Leader to Leader* (Premier issue, 1996), p. 33.
7. John Naisbitt, *Megatrends* (New York: Warner Books, Inc., 1982).
8. D. Quinn Mills, "The Evolving Independent Executive: Bridging the Corporate Generation Gap," *New York Times* (April 7, 1975), p. F3.

Profile: Dennis Bakke of AES Corporation

1. Unless otherwise noted, all quotations are taken from an interview with Dennis Bakke at his corporate headquarters.
2. Suzy Wetlaufer, "Organizing for empowerment: An interview with AES's Roger Sant and Dennis Bakke," Harvard Business Review, 77(1): 110–123, 1999.
3. Ibid.

Chapter 2: The Strongman, Transactor, Visionary Hero, and SuperLeader

1. Some of the text in this chapter is drawn from the Master's research paper ("Five-Star Manager: The Leadership Style of General Dwight D. Eisenhower," Pennsylvania State University, May 1985) written by Joan C. Everett under the direction of Dr. Henry P. Sims, Jr.

2. Dwight D. Eisenhower, *At Ease: Stories I Tell to Friends* (New York: Doubleday & Company, Inc., 1967), pp. 141–42.

3. Ibid, p. 214.

4. All of the quotes and facts about the Coke narrative are taken from *Fortune*, January 10, 2000, pp. 114–116.

5. The information and quotations in this story were taken from Steve Hamm, "Oracle: Why it's Cool Again," *Business Week*. May 8, 2000, pp. 115–126.

6. Ronald A. Heifetz, *Leadership Without Easy Answers* (Cambridge, MA: The Belknap Press of Harvard University Press, 1994), p. 2.

7. This scenario is abridged and adapted from work originally written by Robert Panetta.

8. Richard Branson, *Losing My Virginity* (New York: Random House, 1998), p.31.

9. Des Dearlove, *Business the Richard Branson Way* (New York: AMACOM, 1999), p. 116.

10. Richard Branson, p. 205.

11. Bill Gates, "Bill Gates' New Rules," *Time*, March 22, 1999, p. 74.

Profile: Chainsaw Al—SuperLeader *NOT!*

1. Albert J. Dunlap, *Mean Business: How I Save Bad Companies and Make Good Companies Great* (New York: Fireside, 1996), p.127.

2. Robert Frank and Joann S. Lublin, "Dunlap's ax falls—6,000 times—at Sunbeam," *Wall Street Journal*, November 13, 1998, p. B1.

3. Dunlap, p.131.

4. Frank and Lublin, Op. Cit.

5. Dunlap, p.132.

6. Ibid.

7. Ibid.

8. Joann S. Lublin and Martha Brannigan, "Sunbeam names Albert Dunlap as chief, betting he can pull off a turnaround," *Wall Street Journal*, July 19, 1996, p. B2.

9. Holman W. Jenkins, Jr., "On Net Companies, Milken, and Al," *Wall Street Journal*, April 14, 1999, p. A27.

10. Rick Brooks and Greg Jaffe, "Sunbeam's not so odd couple: Chainsaw Al, Mr. Coffee—triple acquisitions offer CEO Dunlap some familiar turnaround opportunities," *Wall Street Journal*, March 3, 1998, p. B4.

11. John A. Byrne, "How Al Dunlap self-destructed," *Business Week*, July 6, 1998, pp. 58–65.

12. Ibid, p. 60.

13. Martha Brannigan and Joann S. Lublin, "Management: Dunlap faces a fight over his severance pay," *Wall Street Journal*, June 16, 1998, p. B1.

14. Vanessa L. Facenda, "Sunbeam and Dunlap reach accord," *Discount Merchandiser* (September 1998), p. 68.

15. Martha Brannigan, "Best and Worst Performing Companies: Worst 1-year performer: Sunbeam Corporation," *Wall Street Journal*, February 25, 1999, p. R7.

16. Martha Brannigan, "Sunbeam slashes its 1997 earnings in restatement," *Wall Street Journal*, October 21, 1998, p. B6.

17. Online Survey posted on July 18, 1998 at http://www.businessweek.com.

18. Dunlap, p. 133.

19. Nikhil Deigun & Timothy D. Schellhardt, "Some lessons learned from two who felt the axe of Al Dunlap," *Wall Street Journal*, June 23, 1998, p. B1.

20. Dunlap, p. 121.

21. Jenkins, *Wall Street Journal*, April 14, 1999, p. A 27.

22. Brannigan, *Wall Street Journal*, February 25, 1999, p. R7.

Chapter 3: SuperLeadership 101:
The Basics for Unleashing Self-Leadership

1. Robert E. Kelley, *The Gold-Collar Worker* (New York: Addison-Wesley, 1985).

2. See the October 5, 1998 issue of *Forbes* and the feature article, "Management's New Paradigms" by Peter Drucker, pp. 152–176. The quote is on page 164.

3. This procedure is reviewed in the book *Mastering Self-Leadership* (2nd ed.) by Charles C. Manz and Christopher P. Neck (Upper Saddle River, NJ: Prentice-Hall, 1999). The procedure was originally inspired by the classic work of D. Meichenbaum and R. Cameron in their article "The Clinical Potential of Modifying What Clients Say to Themselves," in M.J. Mahoney and C.E. Thoreson, eds., *Self-Control: Power to the Person* (Monterey, CA: Brooks-Cole Publishing Co., 1974).

4. Warren Bennis, "The 4 Competencies of Leadership," *Training and Development Journal* (August 1984), pp. 14–19.

5. For a discussion regarding factors that influence the amount of empowerment allowed followers under differing circumstances, see, *Company of Heroes: Unleashing the Power of Self-Leadership* by Henry P. Sims, Jr., and Charles C. Manz (NY: Wiley, 1986), pp. 150–155.

6. William Serrin, "The Way That Works at Lincoln," *New York Times*, January 15, 1984, pp. 3–4.

Profile: Percy Barnevik of ABB

1. The quotations from Barnevik and de Vries and some of the information in this profile were taken from the article by Manfred. F. R. Kets de Vries, "Charisma in Action: The Transformational Abilities of Virgin's Richard Branson and ABB's Percy Barnevik," *Organizational Dynamics*, (Winter 1998), pp. 7–21; and from original work we reported in *Company of Heroes*, pp. 189–190.

Part II: Self-Leadership Strategies

1. Found in the small book, *Thoughts on Leadership*, part of the Forbes Leadership Library (Chicago: Triumph Books), p. 54.

Chapter 4: Self-Leadership in Action

1. Chapters 3, 4, and 5 in this book are inspired in part by the book *Mastering Self-Leadership: Empowering Yourself for Personal Excellence* (2nd ed.) by Charles C. Manz and Christopher P. Neck (Upper Saddle River, NJ: Prentice Hall, 1999).

2. This example is based on material presented in *Mastering SelfLeadership*, and an earlier article by Charles C. Manz and Charles A. Snyder, "Systematic Self-Management: How Resourceful Entrepreneurs Meet Business Challenges and Survive," *Management Review* (October 1983), pp. 68–73.

3. *Thoughts on Leadership*, p. 92.

4. Private videotaped interview taken from the historical files of Hewlett-Packard, taped August 25, 1980.

Profile: Carly Fiorina of Hewlett-Packard

1. Constance Gustke, "Back to the Future," *Worth* (February 2000), p. 41.

2. Unless otherwise noted, the quotations of Ms. Fiorina were taken from a private interview at University of Maryland, R.H. Smith College of Business. We thank Dr. Ed Locke, Ms. Beth Wade, and Dean Howard Frank for their generosity in facilitating the interview with Ms. Fiorina.

3. This biography is based on HP's homepage (http://www.hp.com).

4. From a commencement speech delivered at Massachusetts Institute of Technology, Cambridge, MA, June 2, 2000.

5. Ibid.

6. Ibid.

7. Ibid.

8. Ibid.

9. Quenten Hardy, "All Carly, All the Time," *Forbes*, December 13, 1999, p. 144.

10. Hardy, p. 141.

11. Gustke, p. 44.

12. Hardy, p. 141.

13. MIT commencement speech.

Chapter 5: Self-Leadership through Natural Rewards

1. Quotes taken from an interview, "That's why they call it 'work'," *Fast Company* (November 1999), p. 194.

2. Chuck Salter, "Rethinking Work," *Fast Company* (April 2000), p. 253.

3. The concept of natural rewards is very similar to the idea of intrinsic rewards. For one viewpoint on intrinsic rewards, see Edward L. Deci, *Intrinsic Motivation* (New York: Plenum, 1975).

4. "Apple's One-Dollar-a-Year Man," *Fortune*, January 24, 2000, p. 76. To be fair, we note that later Jobs was the beneficiary of stock options that produced income of many millions of dollars.

5. "Steve Jobs' Apple Gets Way Cooler," *Fortune*, January 24, 2000, p. 70.

6. *Fast Company* (November, 1999), p. 202.

7. Hans Selye, *Stress Without Distress* (New York: Signet, 1974). Also, see Charles C. Manz and Christopher P. Neck *Mastering Self-Leadership* (2nd ed.) (Upper Saddle River, NJ: Prentice-Hall), 1999, for more discussion on this issue.

8. "The Mobile Century: Work Is What We Do, Not Where We Do It," *Business Week*, June 19, 2000, p. 142.

9. See the cover of *Fortune*, January 24, 2000.

10. S. Kerr, "GE's Collective Genius," *Leader to Leader* (Premier issue, 1996), p. 31.

Chapter 6: Self-Leadership of the Mind

1. Bill Gates with Collins Hemingway, *Bill Gates @ the Speed of Thought* (New York: Warner Books, 1999), pp. 184–185.

2. *Thoughts on Leadership*, p. 58.

3. See, for example, Albert Ellis, *A New Guide to Rational Living* (Englewood Cliffs, NJ: Prentice Hall, 1975).

4. *Thoughts on Leadership,* p. 43.

5. Quotes taken from *Fast Copy* (November, 1999), p. 150.

6. Ibid.

7. Daniel Goleman, "Research Affirms Power of Positive Thinking," *New York Times*, February 3, 1987, p. 15N.

8. Daniel Goleman, *Emotional Intelligence* (New York: Bantam, 1995). Also, for additional information on the subject, particularly as it relates to business and work, see Robert K. Cooper and Ayman Sawaf, *Executive EQ: Emotional Intelligence in Leadership and Organizations* (New York: Grosset/Putnam, 1997).

9. Charles Fishman, "The Way to Enough," *Fast Company* (July-August, 1999), p. 162.

10. Found in Kuki Gallmann, *I Dreamed of Africa* (London: Penguin Books, Ltd., 1991), p. 26.

11. Bill Gates with Collins Hemingway, 1999, p. 185.

Profile: SuperLeadership in the Information Age

1. This profile is based on interviews of managers in large multinational firms that are implementing knowledge-management systems that incorporate elements of the SuperLeadership Approach described in this profile. We have also drawn on published materials obtained from these and other firms.

Part III: SuperLeadership—It's In the Details

1. Kahlil Gibran, *The Prophet* (New York: Alfred A. Knopf, 1923), pp. 64–65.

Chapter 7: Leading Others to Lead Themselves

1. The following story and quotes were found in an article by Matt Murray, "Mentoring Program Turns Underlings Into Teachers of the Web," *Wall Street Journal*, February 15, 2000, pp. B1, B5.

2. An interview with Peter Drucker, "The Shape of Things to Come" *Leader to Leader* (Premier issue, 1996), p. 17.

3. *Thoughts on Leadership*, p. 37.

4. The story and quotes are based on "Learning to Slow Down," *New York Times Magazine*, September 16, 1984, p. 106.

Chapter 8: Leading Individuals to Become Self-Leaders

1. Most of the text in this story is taken from the Master's research paper, "Five-Star Manager: The Leadership Style of General Dwight D. Eisenhower," Pennsylvania State University, May, 1985, written by Joan C. Everett under the direction of Dr. Henry P. Sims, Jr.

2. Stephen E. Ambrose, *Eisenhower: Soldier, General of the Army, President-Elect 1890–1952* (New York: Simon and Schuster, 1983), p. 134.

3. Peter Lyon, *Eisenhower: Portrait of the Hero* (Boston: Little, Brown, and Company, 1984), p. 102.

4. The information and quotes in the following story are taken from: David Streitfeld, "Bill Gates's Executive Style Inspires a Cult Following," *Washington Post*, MAY 1, 2000, pp. A1, A7, A8.

5. Quote from a letter to the editor in *Business Week*, November 26, 1984, p. 9.

6. Private videotaped interview taken from the historical files of Hewlett-Packard, taped March 18, 1981.

7. *Thoughts on Leadership*, p. 92.

8. The quotes in this narrative are taken from *Fast Company* (November, 1999), p. 202.

Profile: Herb Kelleher of Southwest Airlines

1. Katherine Yung, "CEO of Southwest Maintains Zest for Corporate Life," *The Dallas Morning News*, May 14, 2000.

2. Southwest Airlines public relations release, "Southwest Airlines Announces 1999 Profit Sharing Contribution; Employee Sharing Program Helps Raise Corporate Profitability While Fostering Employee Loyalty," *PR Newswire*, March 27, 2000.

3. "Southwest Airlines' Extrovert-in-Chief Named CEO of the Year," *Business Wire*, July 12, 1999.

4. Ibid.

5. Yung, *The Dallas Morning News*.

6. Ibid.

7. J.C. Quick, "Crafting an organizational culture: Herb's hand at Southwest Airlines," *Organizational Dynamics* 21 (2): 45–53, 1992.

8. Yung, *The Dallas Morning News*.

9. "CEO Transforms Southwest Airlines into Reputable Carrier," *Tulsa World*, October 24, 1999.

10. Dan Reed, "Southwest CEO Makes Cancer Announcement with Usual Flair," *Fort Worth Star-Telegram*, August 12, 1999.

11. Quick, p. 45.

12. Yung, *The Dallas Morning News*.

13. Quick, p. 49.

14. Ibid., p. 51.

15. Ibid.

16. Ibid., p. 49.

17. Ibid.

18. Yung, *The Dallas Morning News*.

19. Ibid.

20. Ibid.

21. Kyung Song, "Southwest Airlines Continues to Threaten Rivals with Its Cheaper Prices," *Seattle Times*, November 14, 1999.

Chapter 9: Leading Teams to Self-Leadership

1. Tom Watson, "The Greatest Capitalist in History," *Fortune*, August 31, 1987, p. 29.

2. Private videotaped interview taken from the historical files of Hewlett-Packard, taped August 26, 1980.

3. This information and the quotations are taken from Curtis Sittenfeld, "Power by the People," *Fast Company* (July-August 1999), pp. 178–189.

4. Richard E. Walton, "Work Innovation at Topeka After Six Years," *Journal of Applied Behavioral Science*, 13 (1977): 422–33; Ernesto J. Poza and M. Lynne Markus, "Success Story: The Team Approach to Work Restructuring," *Organizational Dynamics* (Winter 1980), pp. 3–25.

5. This example is based on the chapter "Virtual Teams and Lost Proximity: Consequences on Trust Relationships," written by Joe Nandhakumar and published in *Virtual Working: Social and Organisational Dynamics*, edited by Paul Jackson (London: Routledge, 1999).

6. Philip Evans & Thomas S. Wurster. *Blown to Bits: How the New Economics of Information Transforms Strategy* (Boston: Harvard Business School Press, 2000), p. 212.

7. From Geoffrey Colvin, "Managing in the Info Era," *Fortune*, March 6, 2000, p. F7.

Profile: Joe Paterno & Phil Jackson—SuperLeadership in Sports

1. Unless otherwise noted, Paterno quotes are taken from a personal interview in Paterno's office.

2. Mervin D. Hyman and Gordon S. White, Jr., *Joe Paterno: Football My Way* (New York: Collier Books, 1971), pp. 266–267.

3. Quoted in "Scream Machine at Penn State" by Malcom Moran, *New York Times*, October 10, 1994, p. C3.

4. Ibid.

5. Quoted in *No Ordinary Joe: The Biography of Joe Paterno* by Michael O'Brien (Nashville, TN: Rutledge Hill Press, 1998), p. 146.

6. Data and quotes furnished by the Penn State University Sports Information Department, Summer 2000.

7. Quotes are taken from a Bob Costas TV interview with Phil Jackson, msnbc.com, June 20, 2000.

8. *New York Times* quotes taken from "The Good Father," by David Shields, *New York Times Sunday Magazine*, April 23, 2000.

Chapter 10: Leading Organizational Cultures to Self-Leadership

1. S. Kerr, *Leader to Leader*, p. 30.

2. From John A. Byrne, "The Horizontal Corporation," *Business Week*, December 20, 1993, pp. 76–81.

3. Philip Evans and Thomas S. Wurster, *Blown to Bits: How the New Economics of Information Transforms Strategy* (Boston: Harvard Business School Press, 2000), p. XI.

4. Found in James M. Citrin and Thomas J.Neff, "Digital Leadership," *Strategy 18*, (First Quarter 2000), p. 45.

5. The information and quotes from this story are taken from an article, "What are you working on?" *Fast Company* (April 1999), pp. 112–119.

6. T.E. Deal and A.A. Kennedy, *Corporate Culture* (Reading, MA: Addison-Wesley, 1982); and H. Schwartz and S.M. Davis, "Matching Corporate Culture and Business Strategy," *Organizational Dynamics* (Spring 1981), pp. 30–48, and more recently, Evans and Wurster.

7. These quotes were taken from the case, "Strike in Space," by Balbaky and McCaskey, Harvard Business School, #1-481-008, copyright 1980 by the President and Fellows of Harvard College, and based on the account by Henry F. S. Cooper, Jr., *A House in Space* (New York: Holt, Rinehart & Winston, 1976).

8. From Geoffrey Colvin, "Managing in the Info Era," *Fortune*, March 6, 2000, p. F9.

9. Evans and Wurster, *Blown to Bits*.

10. Peters and Waterman, *In Search of Excellence*.

11. Robert H. Waterman, Jr., *The Renewal Factor* (New York: Bantam Books, Inc., 1987).

Profile: (More) Dennis Bakke of AES Corporation

1. Unless otherwise noted, all quotations are taken from an interview with Dennis Bakke at his corporate headquarters.
2. Suzy Wetlaufer, "Organizing for empowerment: An interview with AES's Roger Sant and Dennis Bakke," *Harvard Business Review*, 77(1): 110–123, 1999.
3. Ibid.
4. "AES's Dennis Bakke: A Reluctant Capitalist," *Business Week Online*, December 13, 1999.
5. Birchard, Bill, "Power to the people," *CFO*, 11(3): 38–43 (Boston, MA).
6. Wetlaufer, 1999, Op. Cit.
7. *Business Week Online*, Op. Cit.

Part IV: SuperLeadership in the 21st Century

1. Quote from interview with Marcus Bullingham and Curt Coffman, "The Great Workplace Secret: It's the Leader Stupid," *Fortune*, October 25, 1999, p. 366.

Chapter 11: Leadership: A Hero or Hero Maker?

1. This story is fictional, but Shervin Pishevar, Drew Morris, and WebOS are all real. The story was inspired by an article from *Fortune*, "Help, I'm the New Boss," May 29, 2000, p. 281.
2. Most of the information and quotations for the Nokia story are taken from Justin Fox, "Nokia's secret code," *Fortune*, May 1, 2000, pp. 161–174.
3. "The Information Technology 100," *Business Week*, June 19, 2000, p. 140.
4. Fox, p. 170.
5. Charles Fishman, "The Way to Enough," *Fast Company* (July-August 1999), p. 166.
6. Ibid.
7. Quote from Curtis Sittenfeld, "Power by the People," *Fast Company* (July-August 1999), p. 180.

Index

About the Authors

DRS. CHARLES C. MANZ AND HENRY P. SIMS, JR., are both speakers, consultants, and best-selling business authors. Their previous books together include *Business Without Bosses: How Self-Managing Teams Are Building High-Performing Companies* (Wiley, 1993, 1995); *SuperLeadership: Leading Others to Lead Themselves* (Prentice-Hall, 1989; Berkley, 1990); *Company of Heroes: Unleashing the Power of Self-Leadership* [Sims & Manz] (Wiley, 1996); *Teamwork and Group Dynamics* [Stewart, Manz, & Sims](Wiley, 1999). Their books have been featured selections for book clubs; translated into several languages, including Japanese, Swedish, Spanish, Indonesian, Korean, Chinese, Portuguese, and German; and also featured on several audiotapes. They are the winners of the prestigious Styble-Peabody literary prize.

In addition, Dr. Manz has written or co-authored *Mastering Self-Leadership: Empowering Yourself for Personal Excellence* (Prentice-Hall, 1992; 2nd edition, 1999); *For Team Members Only: Making Your Workplace Team Productive and Hassle-Free* (AMACOM, 1997); *The Leadership Wisdom of Jesus: Practical Lessons for Today* (Berrett-Koehler, 1998); and *The Wisdom of Solomon at Work: Ancient Virtues for Living and Leading Today*: (Berrett-Koehler, 2001).

Dr. Sims has also written or coauthored: *The Thinking Organization* (Jossey Bass, 1986) and *The New Leadership Paradigm* (Sage, 1992).

Drs. Manz and Sims have served as speaker, consultant, or executive development facilitator for many organizations, including 3M, Ford, Motorola, Xerox, the Mayo Clinic, Procter & Gamble, General Motors, American Express, Arthur Anderson, Allied Signal, Unisys, Josten's Learning, Marriott, Banc One, the American Hospital Association, the American College of Physician Executives, U.S. A.I.D., and the U.S. and Canadian governments.

Dr. Manz is currently the Charles and Janet Nirenberg Professor of Business Leadership in the Isenberg School of Management at the University of Massachusetts. Dr. Manz's work has been featured on radio and television and in the *Wall Street Journal*, *Fortune*, *U.S. News & World Report*, *Success*, and several other national publications. He received the prestigious Marvin Bower Fellowship at the Harvard Business School, which is awarded "for outstanding achievement in research and productivity, influence, and leadership in business scholarship."

Dr. Sims is currently Professor of Management & Organization, The R.H. Smith School of Business, University of Maryland. He has published over 110 research and managerial articles. In 1981, his seminal commentary on self-managed teams was prominently summarized in a feature interview in *U.S. News & World Report*. He has extensive overseas experience, including serving as Fulbright Fellow in Hong Kong.

hsims@rhsmith.umd.edu

cmanz@som.umass.edu

Berrett-Koehler Publishers

BERRETT-KOEHLER is an independent publisher of books, periodicals, and other publications at the leading edge of new thinking and innovative practice on work, business, management, leadership, stewardship, career development, human resources, entrepreneurship, and global sustainability.

Since the company's founding in 1992, we have been committed to supporting the movement toward a more enlightened world of work by publishing books, periodicals, and other publications that help us to integrate our values with our work and work lives, and to create more humane and effective organizations.

We have chosen to focus on the areas of work, business, and organizations, because these are central elements in many people's lives today. Furthermore, the work world is going through tumultuous changes, from the decline of job security to the rise of new structures for organizing people and work. We believe that change is needed at all levels—individual, organizational, community, and global—and our publications address each of these levels.

We seek to create new lenses for understanding organizations, to legitimize topics that people care deeply about but that current business orthodoxy censors or considers secondary to bottom-line concerns, and to uncover new meaning, means, and ends for our work and work lives.

See next page for other books from Berrett-Koehler Publishers

More books from Berrett-Koehler

Berrett-Koehler Publishers PO Box 565, Williston, VT 05495-9900
Call toll-free! **800-929-2929** 7 am-12 midnight

Or fax your order to 802-864-7627
For fastest service order online: **www.bkconnection.com**

Managing By Values

Ken Blanchard and Michael O'Connor

Based on over twenty-five years of research and application, *Managing by Values* provides a practical game plan for defining, clarifying, and communicating an organization's values and insuring that its practices are in line with those values throughout the organization.

Hardcover, 140 pages, 1/97 • ISBN 1-57675-007-8 CIP
Item #50078-353 $20.00

Audiotape, 2 cassettes/3 hrs. • ISBN 1-57453-146-8
Item #31468-353 $17.95

Empowerment Takes More Than a Minute

Ken Blanchard, John Carlos, and Alan Randolph

Empowerment Takes More Than a Minute shows managers how to achieve true, lasting results in their organizations. These expert authors explain how to empower the workforce by moving from a command-and-control mindset to a supportive, responsibility-centered environment in which all employees have the opportunity and responsibility to do their best. They explain how to build ownership and trust using three essential keys to making empowerment work in large and small organizations.

Paperback, 125 pages, 1/98 • ISBN 1-57675-033-7 CIP
Item #50337-353 $12.00

Hardcover, 1/96 • ISBN 1-881052-83-4 CIP • Item #52834-353 $20.00

Audiotape, 1 cassette/90 minutes • ISBN 1-56511-271-7
Item #12717-353 $13.00

The 3 Keys to Empowerment
Release the Power Within People for Astonishing Results

Ken Blanchard, John Carlos, and Alan Randolph

This user-friendly action guide examines and expands on the three keys to empowerment originally presented in Empowerment Takes More Than a Minute-sharing information with everyone, creating autonomy through boundaries, and replacing the hierarchy with teams. It provides managers with thought-provoking questions, clear advice, effective activities, and action tools that will help them create a culture of empowerment.

Hardcover, 200 pages, 5/99 • ISBN 1-57675-060-4 CIP
Item #50604-353 $20.00

Berrett-Koehler Publishers PO Box 565, Williston, VT 05495 9900
Call toll-free! **800-929-2929** 7 am-12 midnight

BK Or fax your order to 802-864-7627
For fastest service order online: **www.bkconnection.com**

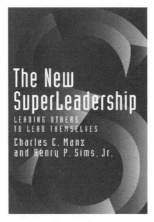